D0564510

B

Shining Through

pulling it together after sexual abuse

by Mindy B. Loiselle and Leslie Bailey Wright

Safer Society Press

PO BOX 340 • BRANDON, VERMONT 05733-0340

Original Copyright © 1992
Mindy Loiselle and Leslie Bailey Wright
Second Edition © 1997

All rights reserved. No part of this publication may be reproduced, stored in a retrieval system, or transmitted in any form or by any means, electronic, mechanical, photocopying, recording, or otherwise without prior written permission of the copyright owners, except for brief quotations included in a review of the book.

Design: Holly McGovern, Whitman Communications Group

Editor: Euan Bear

ISBN: 1–884444–39–3

$16.00
Bulk discounts available.
Phone orders accepted with Mastercard or Visa.

Order from:
The Safer Society Press
P.O. Box 340
Brandon, VT 04733
(802) 247–3132

Acknowledgments

Our sincere thanks to all of the people who have inspired and assisted us in making both the first and second editions of this book possible. They include: Kathy Snowden for her excellent feedback on an early draft; Peggy Siegel for an educator's and children's author's viewpoint; Carol Roper for her feedback and encouragement; David Calof for his dedication to survivors and for his feedback on the second edition; Halceone Bohen for her commitment to empowerment; Sue Drzal for her tireless retypes; Liz Whitehurst for her editorial skill; Marilyn Van Derbur for her powerful presence, role-modeling for success, and moving responses to the second edition; and all the girls and parents whose feedback on the first edition has proven so helpful in shaping the second.

Thanks to Rob Freeman–Longo and Euan Bear for their hard work and for having faith in ours.

To our husbands Lanny R. Levenson and Randy Wright for their good-humored support and encouragement over the long haul.

Lastly, to all the girls and young women who couldn't help but to be an inspiration. We dedicate this book to them.

About the Authors

Mindy Loiselle is a licensed clinical social worker. She divides her professional time between her private practice and her work as an adjunct professor of social work at the Virginia Commonwealth University. Her personal time is spent with her husband, her labrador retriever, and her garden.

Leslie Wright has worked in a variety of inpatient and outpatient settings as a licensed clinical social worker. She received her MSW from Virginia Commonwealth University in 1983. She now lives in Richmond with her husband and three young children.

Publisher's Thanks

The Safer Society Press acknowledges the contribution of the skilled, caring professionals who read this work in manuscript and contributed to its final form: Ellen Bass, Steven E. Mussack, and Lyn Sanford. Without their work, fewer survivors of sexual abuse would move on to thriving lives, and our task of finding, evaluating, and publishing materials to help survivors on their journeys would be much more difficult.

Contents

How To Use This Book

If you are reading this book, chances are that you have been sexually abused. We are sorry this has happened. The best way we know how to help is to write this book. We hope that reading it and trying out some of our suggestions will help you and perhaps your friends and family. Sexual abuse is a frightening experience in any person's life, and you deserve help in dealing with it.

There are some words in the book that you may not know. We use these words because you'll probably hear other people use them and we want you to understand them. We know that even when you do feel ready to talk about what happened, it's hard to find the right words. Since it helps to have words about what happened to you, we will try our best to give a clear explanation of any unfamiliar words.

Most of the time we will speak to you as a girl. Many boys are also sexually abused. If you are a boy reading this, we think it can be useful to you also. But you might want to look for a copy of *Back on Track,* a book we wrote especially for boys who have been sexually abused.

Most of the time, we also talk about the sexual abuser as "he," although sexual abusers are often girls or women. If the person who abused you is a girl or woman you can just say "she" instead of "he." And while we usually talk about adult abusers, we know that kids are often abused by other kids.

We hope you read this book in the way that works best for you. You may want to read a little at a time or all of it at once. The most important thing is that you notice your feelings. If you are feeling curious and interested—keep reading. If you are feeling worried or scared—stop, and come back to it later. It would be best if you have an adult you trust to share your ideas and feelings about the book with. If an adult gave you this book, that person may be a good start. Other possibilities include teachers, guidance counselors, aunts, uncles, or a sponsor from a 12 step program. If all else fails and you feel upset, depressed, or scared when reading this book, call a friend or a hotline. It's important that you have someone to talk to about how you feel.

At the end of each chapter you'll see something called:

helpful things to do

When people who have been abused find ways to feel better inside themselves, they feel stronger. This "Helpful Things To Do" section suggests things you can do to develop more of these "inside yourself" ways of helping. These suggestions will be listed under **journal time, inside time, or imagery.**

journal time: A journal is a safe book to fill with what's on your mind and what you feel. It's like a diary but you can also put in drawings or whatever you like. Get a book with blank pages or a wire-bound drawing pad with blank pages; or, use the "Your Space" page at the end of each chapter in this book. You can write or draw anytime you feel like it. Since ideas sometimes come in colors, not words, it might be good to get some colored pens or markers to use. At the end of the chapters, we will give you some journal ideas you may want to try.

You may want to share what you have written or drawn in your journal with a friend or a relative, or you may not. Sharing your journal is YOUR choice. Most important is finding a safe place to leave it when you aren't using it. You might need an adult to help protect it. You may show this page to an adult who might help so they can understand the importance of your journal and the importance of privacy.

inside time: All people (whether they have been sexually abused or not) need inside ways of helping themselves. One great way is helpful self-talk. Self-talk is what we tell ourselves in our minds. It can be about ourselves, other people, or how we see the world. You may have grown up believing certain messages like "It was my fault" or "I'm bad" or "I have to keep the secret or else..." When you hear those messages over and over inside your mind, it's easy to grow to believe them. We know that the opposite is true too. If you say "It's not my fault, at all" or "I am a good person" or "I deserve help with scary secrets," you can begin to believe in those ideas instead. You can decide to replace the messages that make you feel bad with the new messages that can help you feel good. It takes practice. You may have been thinking those negative ideas for awhile, so don't get discouraged if these new ideas and messages take time to sink in.

imagery: Imagery is another way to help yourself inside. Imagery is a way to use your imagination to make pictures in your mind. Your mind is already using your imagination every time you think, "I'm worried about..." or "I wonder what she'll say..." This kind of imagery has to do with using your mind to make up peaceful, calming, or healing ideas. The images use your senses – sight, hearing, touch, even smell – as many senses as you can use. We include some ways you can use your imagination to help you feel better.

IMPORTANT NOTE:

Different people like different things. All people help themselves in their own special ways. If an idea helps you feel good, use it. If not, don't use it. One day one idea may feel really helpful. The next time you do it, you may not like it. Helping yourself to feel better NEVER happens through force. Experiment gently. Think of this as being like a stream flowing toward the ocean. It takes many twists and turns. Sometimes it stops in a quiet pool beside tall green trees. Sometimes it rushes down a rocky hillside. But it is always moving towards its right and proper place.

a special message

A note for anyone reading this book who is being sexually abused and no one knows yet...

> **TELL!**
> **TELL** a teacher
> **TELL** a police officer
> **TELL** a relative
> **TELL** a neighbor
> **TELL** a friend's parent
> **TELL** your parent...

Just keep telling until someone listens who STOPS the abuse. You will probably not be able to stop it by yourself. We know it's really hard to tell, but it's not good for you to keep this secret. This secret is hurting you right now (even if it doesn't feel like it). You may not always get the kind of help you want when you tell, but telling is the only way to get the help you deserve. Telling is the only way adults can help you be safe. We hope you get the caring help you deserve.

Chapter 1

Something Happened

Something *happened*. It was not your choice. You didn't want it to happen. It was unfair. It should never have happened to you. It was sexual abuse.

We believe you are reading this book right now because you have made a decision. We don't know what that decision was, but we're glad you made it. It could be that you want to know more about sexual abuse, why it happens and who it happens to. Maybe you hope to better understand your feelings about the abuse. You may be looking for ideas about how to deal with these feelings. Or perhaps you're reading this book because someone who knows what happened thought you might be interested.

We believe there are many good reasons to read this book. We hope it helps answer some of your questions. We hope it can give you good ideas about ways to help yourself and ger help from other people. Mostly we hope that by reading it you will feel less alone in dealing with all the feelings the sexual abuse has caused.

We know that making special time to think about what happened to you and your feelings about it is hard. We think you are very brave. If some days reading this book feels too hard, put it down and talk to someone if you can. Come back to it later. Everyone has her own pace.

Though it may not always feel good, we believe you are on the road to healing. Reading a book like this is a good step. What we mean by "healing" is knowing that you are not alone, knowing that the abuser—*not you*—did something wrong, and knowing that no one has any rights or power over you in any sexual way—except you! While there is no quick medicine or cure for healing from sexual abuse, healing and feeling better has happened for many girls and can happen for you.

why me?

There is no good or simple answer to this question. Sexual abuse never should have happened to you. It never should happen to anyone. Statistics show that at least two out of ten girls are sexually abused before they reach the age of eighteen. To think about this another way, if you are one of ten girls in your class at school, there's likely to be at least one other girl in your class who has also been sexually abused. We also know that if there are ten boys in your class, it's likely that one of them has been sexually abused.[1]

Surprised? There is no "outside" way to tell who those other people are. While you sometimes feel like you are the only one facing this problem, you most definitely are not. Unfortunately, sexual abuse of children and young people happens all too often. And it happens in all parts of the world, to girls and boys of all races and religions, and to girls and boys from rich families and poor families and families in between.

Young people are naturally good trusters— they must depend on others. Unfortunately, other people sometimes take advantage of this trust to treat kids in hurtful ways. A person who wants to sexually abuse a young person misuses their trust. To think of this another way, kids are sometimes tricked into going along with sexual touching. It's a trick because often kids don't understand sexual behaviors the way adults or older teenagers do. So once the sexual stuff starts, it's often hard to really understand what is happening. The abuser knew. The kid didn't. It's no wonder kids don't know how to stop it.

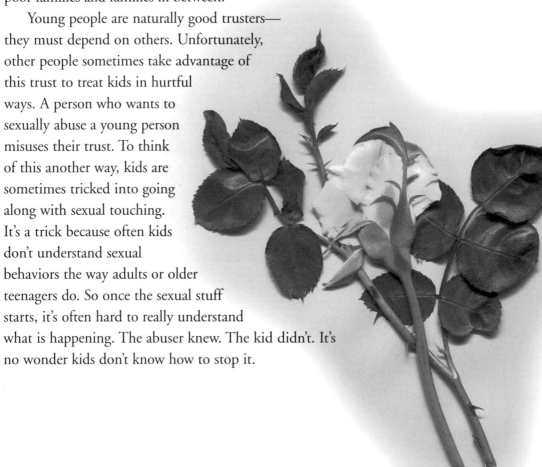

[1] This information comes from a study by Craig Allen, Ph.D., called *Women and Men Who Sexually Abuse Children: A Comparative Analysis*. It was published by The Safer Society Press in 1991.

what is sexual abuse?

Sexual abuse is defined in slightly different ways, depending on who is talking, a lawyer or a counselor. In courts of law, legal definitions are used. Legal definitions of sexual abuse are different in different states. Proving in a court of law that a person was sexually abused by another person is often difficult. Going to court may be necessary and even emotionally helpful, but legal definitions and procedures are not a good measure of the pain and confusion caused by sexual abuse.

So what is sexual abuse? We believe that whenever a kid is tricked, forced, or threatened into sexual behavior of any kind by someone who has more power, it is sexual abuse. When it's an adult, any sexual contact with a child or teenager is abuse. Anyone who has had this type of experience deserves special attention to help them deal with the confused and painful feelings this has caused.

who abuses?

neighbor	uncle	mother	brother
father	minister	babysitter	camp counselor
teacher	cousin	family friend	friend's parent
sister	grandparent	stranger	your friend

Most people do not sexually abuse children, but we think it's important to know that any type of person can be sexually abusive. Unfortunately, people who sexually abuse usually don't look or act any different than other people do. There is no easy way to know who can be abusive. Sometimes kids are abused by more than one person.

While some children are abused by strangers, most are abused by someone they know. Oftentimes it's someone they know and trust. Abusers can do what they do because they have more power than the person they abuse. Adults almost always have more power than children or teenagers, but using power in hurtful ways is not only done by adults. Kids are often abused by other kids.

There are many ways that abusers use their power to take advantage of young people. Some use hitting and threats. They may tell kids that they are bad and the abuse is a punishment. Some blame the kids for the abuse, saying things like "you know you want it to happen." Others threaten by telling kids that all sorts of horrible things will happen if anyone finds out, or that the kids will be in trouble or no one will believe them if they tell about the sexual abuse. All of these threats are made for one purpose—to scare you into keeping the abuse a secret.

Most abusers use niceness to trick kids into sexual touching. They give lots of friendly attention, say nice things, and may even give presents. They may say that sexual touching is an okay way to show love. It may start slowly, with kissing and hugs, and then they trick kids into more and more sexual touching. Since kids are naturally good trusters, abusers use niceness to trick them into trusting them.

We also know that even after other people find out, abusers almost never admit it was their fault. They usually either lie and say the abuse never happened or blame it on the kids they abused. Because abusers don't take responsibility for the things they do, it's even harder on you. Some adults have a hard time believing kids when another adult or older child says they are lying.

If you were abused by a family member, sometimes other family members don't believe you or may blame you. When this happens, counselors say the family is in *denial*. This means someone cannot or will not face the truth. They keep acting like nothing is wrong. If your family is in denial, it is especially important that you have someone you can trust, someone who believes in you. Although it is hard for you not to have the help of family members, we know you can still work toward healing.

If no one in your family can or will help, there are steps you can take to get the help you need and deserve. You should not have to deal with sexual abuse alone. It's just too big a problem for anyone to handle alone. Even adults need help to deal with sexual abuse that happened to them when they were children. All children need and deserve the help of a safe, trustworthy adult.

If you are getting what you need from family members, then it sounds like your family is on its way to healing. If not, here are some ideas about what you can do. Keep trying! (We know it's hard, but we also know that if you have gotten this far, you are really brave.)

some ways to find help

1. Think about who might help you. Is there a teacher, guidance counselor, friend, neighbor, or family member who is nice to you in a way that feels good? Does this person seem like someone you can trust? Tell that person what's going on. If you think it would help, show them this section of the book. If that person does not help, don't give up. Remember, you deserve help. Start thinking about another person who can help.

2. If you have a caseworker or therapist, try your best to tell him or her what's really going on. We know it can be hard to trust others with such important information. You may be scared about what's going to happen if you tell someone you are not being protected or helped in your family. Still, your caseworker or therapist cannot help you or your family unless he or she knows what is really happening. Remember, it's not your job to protect grownups. We know that *saying* this and *feeling* it are two different things. Often, it takes a long time and a lot of thinking about it, feeling about it, and help with it to really know this. But, because we feel so strongly about it we have to say it again: *You need and deserve special help to heal from sexual abuse!*

3. Each city or county should have a number in the phone book you can call to ask questions or to ask for help. It's usually listed under "Social Services" for your city or county. Or you can call Child Help USA. The number is 1-800-4ACHILD or 1-800-422-4453. Calling won't cost anything (and it won't show up on anybody's phone bill—you can even call from a pay phone). They can answer some of your questions and can tell you where to find help in your own area.

so let's remember ...

☼ You didn't want it to happen but because it did, you deserve attention and time to heal.

☼ You are brave to be reading this book and making decisions about healing.

☼ Sexual abuse happens to lots of girls—and boys, too. You are *not* alone!

☼ Every child needs and deserves the help and protection of a safe, trustworthy adult.

helpful things to do

inside time

Once you start to better understand the things you want and need, it may still take a lot of time and practice to make the changes you want to make or to feel comfortable enough to ask others for help. Or maybe you are still working on getting used to the idea that you *can* get help, or that you *deserve* it.

One way to help is to start practicing helpful self-talk. You can choose a special message or several messages that you will say over and over to yourself. Make up one of your own or choose one of these examples.

The sexual touching was not my fault.
I can feel better.
I am a good person.

Now, have you chosen a special message? Try saying it to yourself. You may want to try it in front of a mirror. When you said it, did you notice how it sounded? Did it sound quiet and shaky? That's fine to start. Try it again a little louder and say it like you really mean it. Keep practicing. It's most help-ful if you make special and regular times to say it, like maybe before you go to bed and after breakfast. Some people write their special message on a piece of paper and tape it someplace where only they can see it. It might feel silly at first, but it really helps a lot of people. So, what's your special message?

my special message

_____

_____

_____

Places I'll put my special message to remind myself:

_____

_____

_____

journal time

Writing words down – even when they're someone else's words – helps you claim the feelins for your own. Write these words in your journal or on the lines below:

I need and deserve special help to heal from sexual abuse. It's not my job to protect grown ups.

1. How do you feel when you read these words? What do you think about them? You can write these feelings and thoughts down on the lines below. As you pay close attention to your thoughts and feelings, it may also help to pay special attention to how your body reacts. For example, when you read those sentences listed above, did you notice a knot in your stomach, or did it make you smile, feel tired, surprised, or spaced out? Your body reactions give you good clues to how you feel inside. Come back to these words and keep listening to your inside feelings. Often words like these become more comforatable, more yours, over time.

_____

_____

_____

_____

_____

_____

_____

_____

2. If you grew up thinking it was your job to protect grownups, you may not have had a chance to think about what *you* really need and want. Learning to do that will take a lot of practice. Begin practicing by making up a list of "the things I need to happen." It may help to look at your list every once in awhile to see if some of these things are beginning to happen in your life. Also, the list will probably change. As you begin to have a better understanding of your needs and wishes, the list will help you tell others about what you need.

example

A 10-year-old girl, Beth, was at her uncle's house and he invited her up to his room to watch T.V. While they were watching T.V., he started to talk about sex and then he tried to put his hand on her private parts. Beth told her mother and she and her mother went to a counselor to find out what they should do about the abuse. One thing the counselor did was to ask Beth to write down several things she needed to help her feel better. Beth thought of one thing she needed right now. Think of some other things that Beth might need and write them in the box below.

the things Beth needs to happen

1. *I need a promise from my mother that I'll never be alone with him again.*

2. _____

_____

3. _____

_____

4. _____

_____

5. _____

_____

Fill in the next section for yourself with what you need.

the things I need to happen

1. _____

_____

2. _____

_____

3. _____

_____

4. _____

_____

5. _____

_____

As you think about the things you need, you may find that some of the things you want to put on the list aren't possible—at least for right now. Try making up a "things I wish" list for these things. Even if the things on your list are not possible now, your wishes are important because you can learn a lot about yourself from them. And as you think about your wishes you may be able to come up with some helpful ideas that are possible.

example

One of Beth's wishes was "I wish he wasn't my uncle." Beth decided to share this wish with her mother and her counselor. While they agreed that this was not possible, it helped Beth talk to her mother about her mother's rule of always being nice to family members. They all agreed that sometimes this was not a good rule. They were also able to talk about what Beth could do when she saw her uncle again.

the things I wish would happen

1. _____

_____

2. _____

_____

3. _____

_____

4. _____

_____

5. _____

_____

your space

(Remember, this space is for you to write, draw, or doodle in, to use to express yourself.)

your space

your space

Chapter 2

Why You Told (And Why You Sometimes Regret It)

how the telling about abuse happened

Adults find out in lots of different ways that kids were sexually molested. Telling about being sexually abused usually does not come out right away. Sometimes the girl wanted someone to know for a long time, but didn't know how to tell. Sometimes the girl wanted it buried so deep that no one would ever know—not ever.

Here are the ways some girls and one boy have told about being sexually molested. Maybe you'll see yourself in one of these situations.

She swore no one would ever know, but someone found out.
A friend's father has been kissing and touching Sara in ways she hasn't liked for a long time. She was afraid to say anything. Sara knew she wasn't supposed to go into their house without her parents knowing. She also knew that he's been doing these things to her friend too. One day the friend let out what's been happening and she told about her dad and Sara too. A social worker came to the school and asked Sara if her friend's father touched her sexually and she said "Yes."

She felt bad about what's been happening, but didn't know how to tell.
Juanita's uncle said he wanted to show her something in his room. When she went up there, he made her touch his penis. He said no one would believe her if she said anything, so she never did. When Juanita's mom wanted to go to his house, she didn't want to go, but never said why. One day there was a program at school about secret touching. At the end the leader said, "Has this happened to anyone here?" Juanita raised her hand. (Later she couldn't believe she did it.)

It was so weird she just didn't know what to say.

A teenage babysitter, Darlene, had been taking care of Latoya for a while. Latoya used to think she was really cool and loved to stay with her. But then Darlene started making her play "games" with her that were really weird. She wanted to put things inside Latoya's body. She said it was really grown-up and Latoya was a baby if she didn't want to do it. Latoya felt more and more creepy when Darlene was coming to stay with her and started complaining to her mom about being sick. Then her mom asked why she didn't like Darlene to stay with her any more and she told.

She knew she couldn't say anything because it was too awful. But one day it just slipped out!

Chandra's mom's boyfriend had been putting her to bed. He would hang around when she was putting on her pajamas and she felt nervous and icky. He kissed her too long and when he hugged her, it felt awful. One day her mom was talking about marrying him someday and she felt like she was going to burst! Her mother said, "What's wrong?" She said, "He makes me feel funny." When she asked Chandra why, she told her.

He was talking to a person he knew well and trusted and it slipped out.

Mark had been seeing the school counselor because he hadn't been doing well in school. He used to do fine in school, but lately he'd been mentally "checking out." He began to see the school counselor once a week. One day Mark and she were just talking and she asked, "Has anyone touched you in a way you didn't like?" Even though she had asked him before and he had said, "No" then, this time he told her the truth.

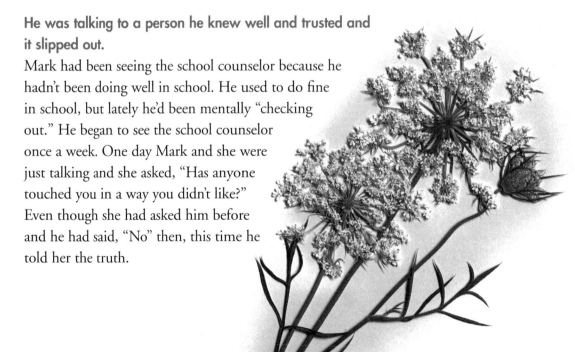

She never wanted it to come out—ever.

Candace's dad has been coming to her bed late at night for as long as she can remember. When he comes, he acts funny—he's very quiet, he doesn't talk and he touches her body in sexual ways. This has been happening more and more. During the day when Candace thought of it, it felt like a dream. But at night she felt very frightened when she went to bed. The waiting and worrying were horrible. She never knew if he would come or not. One day Candace told her best friend and made her swear to keep it secret. But a few days later, a person from Child Protective Services came to her school and asked Candace about what was happening between her and her dad. She was very frightened but she told the person some of what was going on.

You can see from all of these examples that kids usually feel weird about talking about sexual abuse and that it takes a while for the truth to come out.

now people know — why isn't it better?

Sexual abuse is scary for the person it's happening to. It's usually scary for other people too—even people who should help right away. If you have told about being abused, we hope you told a person who helped right away and knew just what to do. A lot of times though, it doesn't happen like that. If the people you told were scared, they probably acted in a way that confused you when you told them. Here are some examples.

they acted angry: Some people act mad when they hear about a child being sexually abused. They raise their voices and may yell. They are yelling because they are upset, and it may have scared you. If this happened when you told, you probably got upset.

scared/worried: Maybe the person you told looked very worried and asked you lots and lots of questions. They may have been questions you could not know the answer to like, "Why did he do that?" or "Why did you let her do that?" If this happened to you, you might feel more worried.

quiet or too calm: Sometimes the people around you can act like nothing has happened. They don't say much, and it may seem like they don't care. It may feel like they are ignoring you. You can feel a lot of ways when people act like this. You might feel better because you think it's all over. You may feel worse because you wonder if they believe you or if they even care about you. Often, if no one talks, it feels too quiet, like these people are *in denial* (see page 16).

doubt or don't believe you: Other people (who don't understand about sexual abuse) are often confused about why the girl didn't tell right away. We know (and want you to know too) that *most* kids don't tell right away for all the reasons we've said. Sometimes (even if you did tell right away) people just don't believe you. They may think you are confused or that someone else made you say this to get revenge on the person you're accusing. They may think you are lying to get someone in trouble or to get yourself out of trouble, or just to get attention. If this happened to you, you probably felt sad, mad, hopeless, and scared.

all mixed up: Often the people in your life may do all these different things. This is especially true when the secret about sexual touching first comes out. Sometimes people are so busy dealing with their own feelings about the sexual abuse that you can't tell what they think or feel about *you*.

a special situation

Sometimes kids feel so bad about how people acted when they told about sexual abuse that they *pretend* they lied about the abuse. The girl may refuse to talk more about it or she might say that what she said before wasn't true. Then the people around her often drop the subject. There are many bad feelings when this happens. The people around the girl think she was wrong to lie. But it is much worse for the girl. She was in a terrible situation when she was alone with a hurtful secret. But now she has lied *about the truth* and the truth keeps on hurting her. We understand why someone does this. If you have thought about doing this—PLEASE DON'T. Healing from sexual abuse is confusing enough.

If you have done this, we understand. It is very common. We hope someday you'll tell someone again. You can also then tell why you pretended it wasn't true before.

what every girl really needs...

☼   Someone who knows and tells you it was good to tell about the abuse.

☼   Someone who knows you're having a bad time right now, but lets you know that it's going to be better.

If your parents are not acting this way, find people who do. If you can't find these people right now, we want you to know:

☼   You were right to tell.

☼   Telling eventually makes it better.

☼   There are ways to help the people around you help you better. We hope reading this book will help you tell others what you need.

helpful things to do

imagery time

Look again at the situations on pages 25, 26 and 27 and pretend for a minute that you could talk to each person. See yourself sitting in a safe place and being able to say anything you think or feel. What do you want to tell them? Write it down.

_____

_____

_____

_____

_____

_____

_____

_____

_____

_____

_____

_____

_____

_____

_____

_____

_____

_____

_____

journal time

Write a short paragraph about how other people found out about your sexual abuse. Look over the feelings list on pages 28 and 29 and write about how different people in your life acted when they found out. Was it like the feelings in the list? Was it hard to tell them at first? Why or why not?

_____

_____

_____

_____

_____

_____

_____

_____

_____

_____

_____

_____

_____

_____

If you are in therapy or counseling, you could write a TV show to tell your therapist how you felt about telling and how you told. You could act it out like you are all the different people, or you could use puppets or dolls. Then make a play about how you *wished* it had happened. Try playing out those different parts.

your space

your space

your space

Chapter 3

Feelings and Secrets

In this chapter we will look at some of the feelings you may have had because of the sexual abuse and because it was a secret. If you felt you could not talk to others about what was happening, you had to deal with your feelings alone. We know you did the best job you could. We also know that being sexually abused causes some pretty big and intense feelings, and that these feelings are difficult to handle alone.

Let's look at some of these feelings.

confusion

Being sexually abused creates many confusing questions and feelings. Did it really happen or could I have dreamed it? How could someone who says he cares about me do this? If adults are supposed to know what's right, why does it feel wrong? Why did this happen to me?

Because the sexual abuse was a secret, you had no one to turn to for help. The only other person who knew was the abuser, and he or she just wanted to make the abuse happen and keep it a secret. This only made it feel worse. Your confused feelings are normal. It's even normal to have opposite feelings at the same time. If the abuser is someone you love, it can make things even more confusing. At times you may be so mad that you wish that person would be thrown in jail forever. Other times, your caring feelings lead you to be nice to that person and to want him to be nice to you. Mostly you wish you could be sure the weird touching would never happen again.

It's okay to not want to think about it on some days and on other days to think about it all the time. It's not unusual if just yesterday you felt scared and alone and today you are so furious you can't stand it. It's okay not to feel the same way about the abuse all the time. The way you feel one day may be completely different the next.

Many girls say their memories and feelings about being abused are fuzzy and unclear. It's not unusual for girls to say that while the abuse was taking place, they "spaced out." This can happen in a lot of different ways. Some girls remember what happened, but say it felt like it was happening to someone else. Some say they remember all the facts about the abuse, but they cannot remember any of the sad, scared, or mad feelings and can't remember why. Since this "spacing out" feeling happens to many girls who have been sexually abused, we'll be talking more about it later in the book.

fear

There are many good reasons why you may have been afraid. Sexual abuse is scary, and so is having to keep the secret. You wanted it to stop, but you could not stop it on your own. You didn't know how to ask for help because you were terrified someone would find out about the secret. The abuser may have threatened to hurt you if you told anyone what was happening. You may have spent weeks, or months, or years feeling too afraid to get help with a problem that you didn't start and you couldn't stop.

If the abuse happened over a long period of time, you may have been scared all the time. You never knew when it could happen again. Nothing you did or didn't do seemed to help. Even if the abuse happened once, it was hard for you to feel safe. Whether it happened once or many times, you probably feared it would happen again.

Sometimes the person who sexually abuses is abusive in other ways too. Hurting a kid's body with mean hitting (physical abuse) or constantly hurting her feelings with mean words (emotional abuse) are also types of abuse. Seeing someone else's body or feelings be hurt on purpose can be just as scary and painful. If you knew about or saw someone else be sexually, physically, or emotionally abused, this probably caused painful feelings that were hard to deal with.

If you have grown up feeling it was your job to protect other people (like younger brothers and sisters), then you may have felt bad because you really couldn't protect them. Sometimes, an abuser may trick a girl into sexual touching by promising not to touch another child, perhaps a younger brother or sister. The girl may go along with the sexual touching, thinking she is protecting someone else. Unfortunately, the abuser's promise often turns out to be a lie, and the abuser still abuses the other children too.

If something like this has happened to you, we want to say this loud and clear: IT WAS NOT YOUR FAULT! Because you were a kid and didn't have as much power as the abuser, you couldn't really protect someone else. It's just not fair that you had to worry about these things. You deserved and needed the help and protection of a grownup, and so did any other children who were abused.

Being sexually abused can also lead to questions and fears about your body. Questions you may have now or thought of in the past might include:

Has the abuse hurt my body? Could something be broken?
Will my body grow normally — the same as other girls?
Am I still a virgin? If not, what does that mean?
If the abuser was a woman, does that make me homosexual?

(You may have heard other words for this term such as gay or lesbian, or queer, dyke, lezzie, or faggot.)

Could I be pregnant?
Can somebody look at me and tell that I was abused?
Is sex always something that hurts people?

We hope you have someone you can talk to about your questions. Sometimes talking to someone about your fears really helps. It may help you feel better if you can be examined by a doctor. A doctor can be a good person to help you feel better about what's going on with your body. Remember, none of your questions are silly or stupid. All of your questions are very important.

shame and guilt

Young people tend to believe that bad things happen to them because they somehow deserved it. The shameful feelings that girls get about being abused are the ones that make them feel like they are bad because the abuse happened or that they are bad because it happened in their families. The guilty feelings are the ones that come when the girl thinks she actually did something to cause the abuse. Some girls feel guilty because they couldn't figure out a way to stop it. Others feel guilty because they were abused while they were breaking a family rule, like going somewhere their parents told them not to.

We hope that by now our ideas about this are pretty clear, but we think it's helpful to hear some things over and over again. We hope you have other people who say it and show it too. You were NOT responsible for being sexually abused. Nothing that you did, said, felt, or thought caused the abuse. The abuser caused the abuse to happen.

In our work with girls who have been sexually abused, we have heard many of the reasons that they have felt guilty. We think it might help you if we share some of the concerns that come up a lot. We will also share why we know it wasn't the girl's fault!

I feel guilty because...

Why it wasn't your fault:

1. I sometimes felt special and cared for by the person who abused me.

Sometimes you may have been treated as special. Attention, nice words, gifts, all make everyone feel good. That does not mean you wanted sexual touching.

2. I didn't find a way to stop the abuse.

Children always have less power than people older than they. Probably nothing you could have done would have stopped the abuse. Girls who fight back often can't stop the abuse. No matter what, it was not your responsibility to stop the abuse.

3. I sometimes had good feelings in my body during the abuse.

Our bodies are built so they can give us good feelings sexually. If the abuse happened a lot, you may have begun to feel pretty sexual. Sexual feelings are not bad. They are natural. Being forced, tricked, or encouraged to have sex before you want or are ready to is what is confusing and hurtful.

4. I was doing something I wasn't supposed to (went to a party, sneaked out to meet someone, drank beer...) when the abuse happened.

Even if you were breaking a family rule, it doesn't mean you deserved sexual abuse. But it does make it harder to tell because you'll probably get in trouble for breaking the rule. You did not deserve to be abused no matter what else you might have done.

5. I didn't say "no."

You couldn't say "no" because...
You had less power.
You were smaller.
You were too scared.
The abuser wouldn't have listened anyway.
The abuser threatened to hurt you if you did.

6. I didn't tell.

Reread Chapter 2!

protective feelings

We often find that girls who have been sexually abused grow up feeling especially protective of other people's feelings. This can mean that they grow up believing that other people's feelings are more important than their own. Because you know what it feels like to be hurt, you may try especially hard not to hurt other people. You may have thought that telling the secret was something that would hurt people you care about.

Caring for others is important, but not if it means you end up being hurt as a result. It's not fair! It's not right! No one should be touched in a sexual way if they don't want to be, and no one should have to keep this kind of secret. If someone asked you to, he or she was not thinking about what's good for you. He was being selfish. You have the right to protect yourself. You also deserve to have the protection and care of a grownup who can help.

We know that sometimes the people you wanted most to say "You did the right thing by telling" can't or won't give you what you need. This makes everything much harder. But it also makes it even more important that you understand it is good to protect yourself.

Even after the abuse is no longer a secret, you may feel protective of other people's feelings. This may lead you to try and show other people that the abuse was "no big deal." We've heard many girls who were trying to protect other people's feelings (including ours) say things like "The abuse is over now, why can't everyone just forget about it?"

We understand that everyone sometimes needs a break from hard stuff—like dealing with sexual abuse. But we also know that the "hard stuff" doesn't go away by itself, and people usually continue to have problems because of the abuse, even after it has stopped. Most girls continue to have strong feelings about the abuse and the abuser for a long time. Probably other people in your life will have strong feelings about the abuse too. We hope they will deal with their feelings and actions so that they can be given a chance to really heal too. But they are the only ones who can make that choice. Your only responsibility is to deal with your own feelings and actions, no matter what else is going on around you.

sadness

Usually people have sad feelings because of the abuse. When people are sad they may feel like crying or like they have lost something important to them. Because you didn't want others to worry about you, and because of the abuse secret, you may have learned to hide your sad feelings. Not being able to show your feelings and be comforted may have made you feel even worse.

When sad feelings become very strong, they are extra hard to deal with. If your sad feelings hurt too much, you may have tried to ignore them or pretend they weren't there. Perhaps this is what you had to do at the time you were being abused.

We believe sad feelings are important ones to pay attention to. We hope you have someone to share them with. There are times when sad feelings get so deep and so large they won't go away without special help from a therapist or doctor. As you share your feelings and spend time thinking about them, there's a good chance you will begin to feel better. But (and we know this is a big "but"), sometimes people feel worse before they can feel better.

If you've had your sad feelings buried deep inside you for a long time, it can be hard when they start to come out. It may not feel like it at the time, but this can be a really good sign. Getting to know your true feelings is a good step toward healing.

anger

Sometimes your angry feelings can scare you. You may worry that showing your anger will make others angry at you. Or perhaps you're afraid you won't be able to control your anger if you let yourself really feel it. Maybe you're confused about how to be angry at someone you also care about. These are all normal worries, but believe it or not, your angry feelings can be good for you.

Often it's the angry part of you that knows the abuser was wrong and that what happened was not your fault. Your anger can give you the courage to say, "It's not my fault."

If your angry feelings sometimes really do feel too big to handle, and if you find that you often do things that you feel bad or scared about when you are mad, you can get help with this. With the help of a caring adult or a therapist, other people have learned to have their angry feelings and feel like they can control them. You can too!

so remember ...

☼ Being sexually abused and keeping it secret causes big, deep, strong feelings that are hard to handle alone.

☼ Sexual abuse is a confusing experience and you won't feel the same way about it every day. Your feelings about the abuse are important and should be treated with respect.

☼ Your feelings are not bad or weird. They are a natural reaction to having an awful thing happen to you—sexual abuse.

☼ With help and time, most people can feel a lot better.

helpful things to do

imagery time

Let's pretend. Use your imagination to pretend that you have a friend who has been sexually abused. What are three messages you would give her that you think could help her? (Example: "You were right to tell.") Write them on the lines below.

_____

_____

_____

inside time

Now, who better deserves a friend than you? (If you are having trouble, we'll give you the answer—nobody.) So, try being a friend to yourself. Using helpful self-talk, try saying those three helpful messages to yourself. Remember that friends care about each other, so give *yourself* some of those caring feelings too.

journal time

Each of the feelings that we talked about in this chapter (**Confusion, Fear, Shame and Guilt, Protective Feelings, Sadness,** and **Anger**) are listed below. Write about a time you recently felt each of these feelings. If you are not used to paying attention to your own feelings, you may have to think hard to remember and be aware of them. Maybe you can try for the next few days to take special time to pay attention to what's inside. Then, come back to your feeling page in the journal and see if you have more to write. Which of these feelings is hardest for you? Easiest? Scariest? Which do you feel you need help with? Are there feelings we have left out? Add them at the end of the list.

example
Protective Feelings

I felt protective last night when I didn't
want my mother to know I had been
thinking about the abuse and I started
to cry. Sometimes I wish I could tell
her so she could hug me and try to
help me feel better.

my feelings about the abuse
Confusion

Fear

Shame and Guilt

_____

_____

_____

_____

_____

_____

Protective Feelings

_____

_____

_____

_____

_____

_____

Sadness

_____

_____

_____

_____

_____

_____

Anger

_____

_____

_____

_____

_____

_____

Other Feelings

_____

_____

_____

_____

_____

_____

your space

your space

your space

Chapter 4

Old Coping / New Coping

In Chapter 3, we looked at some of the feelings you may have had because of the sexual abuse and because it was a secret. We stressed that sexual abuse causes strong feelings that are difficult to handle alone. But, we know that like most girls, you probably did handle these feelings alone. In this chapter, we will look at some of the ways you may have tried to deal with your feelings and help yourself feel safer.

We must say it again—you were brave! You did the best job you could in a terrible situation. Whatever way you tried to help yourself feel better was what you needed to do at the time. You were in an emergency situation and you needed emergency help. But some of the ways you learned to handle feelings might not be helping anymore. Maybe they even get in the way of what you want for yourself.

If changing some of the ways you act and feel is something you want to do, you *can* do it. It won't be easy, and you may need the help of someone you trust and can talk to.

coping

It may be helpful to think of ways of coping as tools for dealing with feelings. As we grow, our feelings and the ways we deal with them also grow. Have you ever seen a young child having a temper tantrum? She was having a hard time coping with the BIG feelings inside her. If we looked inside the young girl's coping toolbox, we could see that she does not yet have many tools to help her deal with her BIG feelings. As she grows, she collects more tools to help her.

When terrible things like sexual abuse happen to kids, they don't have many tools to help them cope. They often develop special emergency tools. Here are some of the emergency tools we have seen many girls use to cope with sexual abuse.

separating yourself from the abuse

When something horrible happens, one way people cope with it is to try and imagine it never happened. Your mind may be so good at this that you may have actually "forgotten" for some time. Even when you do remember the abuse, it may seem more like it was a dream or like it happened to someone else. This was your mind's way of protecting you from feelings that were too big, too strong, too confusing, too painful, and too hard to handle at the time. Counselors call this mind's way of protecting yourself *dissociation* (say "diss-so-see-AY-shun").

Many girls have said that even while the abuse was actually happening, it felt unreal, like a dream, or like it was happening to someone else. Some girls say that it felt like they actually left their bodies while the abuse was happening. Some have said they were afraid to tell their trusted helpers or therapists about this because they thought it might sound "crazy." It's not! It's just a very special emergency tool that some people use when they have to deal with a horrible situation.

"Forgetting" and "dreaming" are emergency tools. In some emergencies they can work well. The problem is that this way of coping can become automatic. You may use it more and more in situations that aren't emergencies. After using these two emergency tools for a while, sometimes people find they can't feel any feelings. Sometimes they get so numb they can't concentrate in school or in other parts of their lives. If this happens to you, then it will probably get in the way of things you want to do. A therapist or counselor can help you change this if that is what you want, and we will talk more about it in Chapter 7 on Therapy.

Using alcohol or drugs is another way that some kids separate themselves from the abuse and the pain it causes. If you are using alcohol or drugs now, or have in the past, it may help to look at this as one way you tried to escape hurting. The problem is that using alcohol or drugs usually leads to many more problems—and even more hurting.

A big part of healing is learning how to deal with feelings. Using alcohol or drugs to numb feelings blocks healing. It will also get in the way of your being able to collect and practice better coping tools.

When people use alcohol or drugs a lot to help them cope, it's often hard to stop. If you want to stop but are not sure you can do it alone—help is available. Talk about it with your counselor or another helpful adult, or look under Alcoholics Anonymous (AA) or Narcotics Anonymous (NA for help with quitting drugs) in your phone book. These groups have helped many people stop using alcohol or drugs. When you call, they should be able to tell you about meetings in your area. Some meetings are for teens only.

thinking abuse is normal and good

When a girl is sexually abused by someone she likes and trusts, she may use another type of special coping: she may tell herself the abuse is okay. Even if she doesn't like the person, learning to think the abuse is okay can make something awful feel much less bad.

example

Alicia's mom married a man who has really helped make their lives better. Since he's been with them her mom is happier and they live in a nice house with a yard, instead of the tiny apartment they had before. Alicia likes seeing her mom happy. She used to be really worried about her family. When her stepdad began to come into her room and touch her sexually, Alicia felt scared and confused, because he was still so nice. She decided that going along with the abuse was a good thing, and she thought it would help her family. She began to like the presents and special attention he gave her. When her mom found out and was so upset, Alicia felt **really** confused.

Learning to think the abuse is okay is one way girls feel more in charge and not so helpless. If the girl feels like this and the abuse is found out and people are upset, she usually feels *really* awful. "Liking" the abuse is a confusing coping skill, but a counselor or therapist can help you understand it.

For some girls it gets even more confusing when some of the sexual touching felt good. It helps to remember that sexual feelings are normal. It doesn't mean that the girl caused or is responsible for the abuse. Chapter 6 will talk more about disconnecting sexual feelings from the abuse.

putting anger in the wrong place

taking it out on others

Sometimes kids who have been sexually abused have learned to deal with some of their feelings by sexually touching other children.

example

Janice, who had been sexually abused when she was younger, was babysitting for the three-year-old boy down the street. While she was giving him a bath she remembered her own abuse and she felt icky inside. She got the idea of rubbing the little boy's penis, and she did.

Sometimes sexually touching other children can be a way to express angry feelings. It can be the girl's way of saying, "Someone hurt me, so I'll hurt someone else." Other times, sexual touching may be the only way a girl has learned to express caring feelings, because this is what she was taught by the person who abused her.

Sexual feelings and being curious about sex are normal and good. Encouraging or forcing someone into sexual touching who doesn't want it or understand it is not good for anyone. Kids you might be touching sexually will be confused and hurt the same way you were. If you are doing this kind of sexual touching, you need to stop. If you have learned to express your feelings with sexual touching, you can learn to stop as you learn to know and talk about your own painful feelings about when you were abused. With help, you can learn to express your loving and angry feelings in ways that are safe for you and for others.

If you are worried about any sexual touching you have done to other people in the past, please talk about this with your counselor or therapist. This person should be understanding, and they can help. You don't need to be by yourself with this.

You probably have questions about what will happen if you tell a therapist about any unwanted sexual touching you have done with other kids in the past. Perhaps it will help to show the therapist this part of the book. Ask him or her to talk to you about what usually happens when a girl or boy tells about sexually touching another kid who doesn't want or understand it. Some good questions may be ...

1. Do you have to tell this to anyone else?

2. If you do, what happens then?

3. Will you be there to help me straighten this all out?

The answers to these questions will depend on several things. You and your therapist will figure this out together. The main goal is to get the unwanted sexual touching to stop. That's what's best for everybody.

taking it out on yourself

Kids often believe that when bad things happen to them, it must have been because they deserved it. If you felt this way, it may have led you to be angry and sad with yourself. At the time, it probably was not safe to express your anger at the abuser or other people you were angry with, so you may have taken this anger out on yourself.

example

Maddy had been told over and over by the person who sexually abused her that she was bad. Maddy began to believe it. Although she had really liked school before, she found herself disobeying the teacher on purpose. It was strange, but it kind of felt good to get in trouble. She figured that since she was bad, she might as well act that way. Just like "forgetting," this is actually an emergency tool that can help for awhile.

We hope that at this point in your life, you are working hard at knowing that the abuse was not your fault, and that *you* don't deserve that anger at yourself. You do deserve special time and attention to heal. One part of healing is being and feeling safe enough to put your anger where it belongs.

You have a right to be angry at the abuser. You have a right to be angry at the people who couldn't or wouldn't protect you. And, it's okay to be angry—very angry—even at people you care about.

We believe your angry and sad feelings deserve special attention, and it's important to find ways to safely express them. When these feelings are not given attention, they can get stronger and stronger. There are many warning signs that let us know our feelings have become too big for us to handle alone. We will list them, but please remember that each girl handles her feelings differently. If you think your feelings are too big to handle alone, it's important to find someone to help you safely deal with them.

WARNING SIGNS
That Your Feelings Are Too Big To Handle Alone

Put a checkmark or an X in the box next to the questions you would answer "Yes."

☐ Have you gained or lost a lot of weight recently?

☐ Do you feel like eating all the time? Are you overeating and then feeling bad about it? Do you sometimes "space out" and not notice how fast or how much you are eating?

☐ Do you ever make yourself throw up?

☐ Are you skipping meals a lot, eating two bites and throwing the rest away, or not eating at all?

☐ Has the way you sleep changed? Do you have trouble falling asleep? Do you wake up during the night? Do you want to sleep all the time? Do you have a lot of nightmares?

☐ Are you always feeling unlovable, unloved, and like you can't do anything right?

☐ Do you feel tired all the time? Or do you feel like you have too much energy and you can't concentrate or relax?

☐ Do you cry often, even when you're not sure what's wrong?

☐ Do you sometimes feel like life's not worth it? Have you thought about dying? Do you sometimes wish you'd never been born?

☐ Do you ever want to or have you ever hurt your own body on purpose (burns, cuts, bruises or hitting, and so on)?

☐ Do you often put yourself in dangerous situations? Have you run away from home? Have you been sexually active without knowing if you really want to be?

☐ When you are angry or feeling bad, do you do things that hurt other people? Are you afraid you might?

☐ Are you having a hard time concentrating at school or while doing your homework? Have your grades gone down?

☐ Are you using alcohol or drugs?

☐ Have you recently begun to smoke or increase your smoking?

☐ Do you get angry easily over little things that didn't bother you in the past?

☐ Have you "borrowed" anything without permission and not given it back? Have you shoplifted candy, clothes, makeup, cd's or other things from stores?

☐ Have you felt like touching or have you touched someone else's body sexually who didn't want you to or who was too young to understand or say no?

☐ Do you think the only good thing about you is that you know how to be sexy? Do you only remember good things when you remember sexual abuse?

☐ When you masturbate, or touch yourself sexually, for your own pleasure, do you think about the abuse?

☐ Do you touch or rub your private parts for so long and so hard it hurts? Do you rub or touch your private parts where people notice it and get upset with you (in school, in church, in other public places)?

☐ Are there other things you do when you feel bad or lonely that might get you in trouble if other people knew about them? What are they?

_____

_____

_____

If you've checked any of the items on this list, remember you are not alone. Many other girls who have been sexually abused have felt these feelings or done these things. It's important that you talk with someone who can help. If you don't have someone to talk to yet, and you have checked things on the list, please find a therapist or counselor because these are signs that you do need help. (Remember, at the end of Chapter 1 we suggested ways to find the help you need. Also, Chapter 7 will talk about what it's like to work with a therapist.) If you don't know how to talk about these things, show the person who is helping you the list with your checkmarks on it.

Ignored feelings never just go away. Feelings may be buried deep inside us, but they are still there waiting for us to find them. Our hearts and minds have to find ways to cope with them. Again, some of the ways you've learned to cope may not be helping anymore, even though they helped for awhile. But dealing with sexual abuse does not make it okay to do things that are wrong or that hurt other people. Knowing that you might have done some of these things because of your feelings about being sexually abused means that it is easier to understand. When you get help with your feelings, you'll learn new ways of coping. We know too that it can be scary and hard to change and learn other ways to cope. Healing takes time.

We believe you've continued to read this book because you are interested in healing. We want you to think about what that means again. Healing is knowing that you are not alone, knowing that the *abuser* did something wrong and not you, and knowing that no one has any rights over you in any sexual way—except you!

so remember ...

☼ Because of sexual abuse, you may have invented and used emergency coping tools.

☼ These coping tools have often helped in the past, but may not be helping now.

☼ You can learn new coping tools. Everyone needs lots of ways to cope.

☼ If you don't feel safe yet, it's important to tell people so you can be safe and feel safer—safe enough to be in charge of your life again and on the road to healing.

helpful things to do

journal time

1. Write about some of the "emergency tools" you used to help you cope with sexual abuse. Do you still use them now? When? How does it affect your life? Does it help sometimes? When does it get in the way of what you want? Are there things about the way you cope that you want to change?

_____

_____

_____

_____

_____

_____

_____

_____

_____

_____

_____

_____

_____

_____

_____

_____

_____

_____

_____

_____

_____

_____

_____

2.

If there are things you want to change, list some helpful ideas about how you can do it. This may be a good time to show your ideas to someone you trust. Maybe that person can help too.

example:

I'm going to try to really notice when I feel myself beginning to "space out."

(1.) I will write in my journal the times I notice myself "spacing out."

(2.) I will go back and read about the times that "spacing out" happens. I will look to see if there's a pattern in when and why it happened at those times.

(3.) Talk to my special helper and see if she can help me figure out any patterns.

what I want to change & my plan for changing it

_____

_____

_____

_____

_____

_____

_____

_____

_____

_____

_____

_____

_____

_____

_____

_____

_____

_____

your space

your space

Chapter 5

Choosing Your Own Road

As we wrote in earlier chapters, sexual abuse usually causes a crisis or emergency situation in a person's life. You probably got bumped off the road you were on in life. Dealing with the abuse and the fact that it was a secret takes up a lot of energy that you should have been able to use for other things, like making friends, learning, and doing things you enjoy. Like for most kids who were abused, how you feel about yourself and about your relationships with other people probably changed for the worse. In this chapter, we'll look at some of the ways this happens. We'll also look at how you can begin to change these negative feelings and make your own choices about what you want in life.

how abuse lowers self-esteem

If you look up the word "esteem" in *Webster's New World Dictionary*, you'll find this: "to value highly, respect." Esteem is the positive way you feel about someone you admire. Self-esteem is the deep-down feeling that you really are an okay person. It's the amount of respect you have for yourself. Most people start out life with that okay feeling of self-esteem. But you can get bumped off the good self-esteem road and into the ditch of low self-esteem when bad things happen, especially when someone you care about hurts you on purpose.

Most kids feel worse about themselves after being abused than they did before it happened. Sexual abuse often lowers a person's self-esteem. When you don't feel like you're worth very much, that's low self-esteem. When bad things happen, kids usually feel like they deserved it—unless there are caring people around to show them the truth: they did not deserve it and it was not their fault! When you believe the sexual abuse was your fault, the negative thoughts and feelings you have about the abuse get connected to your thoughts about yourself.

Sexual abuse is not the only thing that can injure a person's feelings about herself. Some things that make people feel bad about themselves are not such a big deal—in a few days or weeks you get over them and feel okay again. Other things are really big deals and stay with a person for a long time. Sexual abuse is usually one of the big things.

Some kids who are sexually abused have to deal with other big things too. Another way a person's self-esteem can be injured is by being physically hurt on purpose (being hit, kicked, thrown against a wall, or hurt by a weapon), especially by someone who is supposed to care. This is physical abuse. Still another way self-esteem can be injured is when a parent or other important people call a person names a lot of the time, such as telling her she's worthless or stupid or fat or ugly. This is emotional abuse.

Sometimes the abuser says things that teach kids to believe they are bad or that they caused the abuse. Even when there are no out-loud messages, kids find ways to try to explain this bad experience to themselves. According to some kids we've talked to, their thoughts sound something like this:

"She hits me because I'm bad."

or

"He molested me because of the way I look and dress."

or

"They hate me because I'm stupid."

There are a lot of negative messages that you may tell yourself to try to make sense of the abuse. This is called "negative self-talk." It's another way a person tries to make sense of what's happening. Unfortunately you may hear these types of messages from other people, too, from family members, on TV, from kids at school. They may not even be talking about you or your situation, but the messages are still there:

"I'll beat some sense into you," says mom.

or

"You could do it if you weren't so stupid and clumsy," says stepdad.

or

"Anyone who isn't a virgin when she gets married is a slut," says a friend.

or

"Look at the way those girls are dressed—they were just asking to be raped!" says someone on a talk show.

When you hear these kinds of messages often enough, it's likely that you begin to believe them. Then you may begin to say these things to yourself, too.

steps to choosing your own road

If your self-esteem has been injured because of abuse, we'd like to say something loud and clear: You Don't Deserve It! The truth is, no one deserves it. Fortunately, you can change your self-esteem if you want to, just as other kids have. And that's something worth working for. Where do you begin? You already have begun by taking positive steps like reading and working through this book. It's important that the negative thoughts and feelings you now have about yourself be reconnected with what caused them in the first place: the abuse. Then you can begin to work on connecting more positive thoughts and feelings with what they should be connected with: you. This is a part of the work you've already been doing.

changing self-talk

Self-talk is what you say to yourself (not out loud but in your mind) about yourself, other people, and the world. It can be positive or negative. One big step to building up your self-esteem is changing the negative self-talk you've learned back into positive self-talk. We know this is not a simple step, especially if you've been thinking negative self-talk for a long time. You may not even realize you're doing it. It will take some real effort and concentration to figure out what messages you've been giving yourself.

To change negative self-talk into positive self-talk, first start listening to your thoughts. Some messages are connected with the abuse ("It's my fault," or "I deserved it."). Usually negative self-talk begins to creep into other areas of your life, too. When you're meeting someone new, you might hear yourself thinking, "I know she won't like me." Or when you think about trying something new, you might catch yourself thinking, "I could never do that." If your self-talk sounds like these messages, you're talking yourself out of enjoying or accomplishing many of the things you really want to do. You've been bumped off your own road into a ditch, and it's pretty hard to get anywhere when you're stuck in a ditch.

catching that thought

The first step in changing negative self-talk is to catch yourself doing it. Usually these thoughts just float by in the back of your mind without your noticing. You may feel the sad, mad, awful, lowdown feelings that go with the thoughts, but you don't realize there are words that started the feelings.

One way to catch that thought is to keep a piece of paper in your pocket. Make a mark on the paper every time you hear yourself thinking something negative or bad about yourself. The next step is to write down the negative thought as soon as you realize you're thinking about it.

example

When Megan counted her negative self-talk thoughts, at first she only caught two or three per day. By the second Thursday, though, she was shocked to find out that she had 13 negative thoughts! She decided that probably that meant she was good enough at catching the thoughts, so she went on to writing them down. When she read them over, she realized how familiar they all sounded. "I'll never get anybody to like me," was one. "I can't ever dress right, I'm such a slob," was there on a day when she wore new jeans, a turtleneck and a new sweater. "You can't hurt me—I'm already bad," was another. After a couple of weeks keeping track of her negative thoughts and looking at what they said, she was ready for the next step: replacing them!

replacing the message

Replacing the message means thinking of new, positive, true things to say to yourself instead of the negative things. Sometimes kids start by thinking of words that contradict, or counter, the negative thoughts they'd been having.

example

Megan started countering her negative thoughts. Whenever she caught herself thinking, "I'll never get anyone to like me," she mentally said "STOP! I have friends who like me and I'm a likable person." When the negative thought was, "You can't hurt me, I'm already bad," she practiced thinking, "I don't want to be hurt, I don't deserve to be hurt, I'm a good person that someone did something bad to."

Think about some positive, encouraging, true words you can say to yourself the next time your negative self-talk comes up. Think of what you might say to a good friend who was down on herself, then be that friend for yourself. What's your new message? Trying saying it out loud. Write it down. Put it on a little sticky note or a piece of paper and tape it inside your purse or a notebook where you'll see it every day. Think about how it feels to say the new message. Talk to someone else about it if you want to. For most kids, the new messages take time to sink in. It takes practice. Make a plan for when you'll practice it, and then do it several times a day. It may feel weird or silly at first, but positive self-talk has helped many kids (and adults too!).

putting words into action

Replacing negative messages with positive ones is a good step, but it won't work in the long run unless your actions fit the words. You won't feel better about yourself if you often do things that make you feel guilty, ashamed, angry, or sad. A lot of kids need to work on not feeling guilty for the things they're not responsible for—like the abuse, for example, or a divorce. But at the same time, feeling guilty, ashamed, angry, and sad is a normal response when kids knowingly do things that hurt themselves or others—like lying, using drugs, drinking, shoplifting, or having unprotected sex with a lot of partners they don't really care about, for example. These feelings give you the message that something is not right, something needs to change. No one can really feel good about herself until she takes responsibility for her own actions. And you are not responsible for anyone's actions but your own.

be willing to try

All of us have things we are good at. Find yours. We all have certain strengths, talents, and gifts to share. But you can't know what it feels like to be good at something unless you try it. It's okay to try something new and then find out that you're not good at it or that you don't really like it. It's definitely okay to try something new and let yourself not be good at it in the beginning until you learn how. It helps you learn more about yourself, and you can be proud of yourself for trying. The world needs your gifts, and you need to share what's inside you.

relationships after the abuse

We wrote in the chapter on feelings about how being sexually abused can make you feel alone, isolated, and different. This may be a good time to think about your own reactions to the abuse and how they have affected your relationships with others. Do you have a hard time trusting anyone else? Have any of your close relationships with family members or friends changed since the abuse? Are you spending more time alone? Making excuses not to hang out with or talk to people you used to like?

If you're having trouble trusting or being close to others since the abuse, it's understandable. Many girls do. Your sense of trust has been injured by the abuser. Being cautious about who to trust is wise, but at the same time, many kids (and adults) don't really feel good about themselves if they don't feel connected to people.

On the other hand, does being alone feel too scary since the abuse? Do feelings and thoughts about the abuse come up when you're alone that you wish would go away? Are you finding excuses to hang out with people, ANY people, even people you wouldn't have wanted to hang out with before the abuse? To fit in with these people are you doing scary, dangerous things (like trying drugs or unprotected sex)?

Not wanting to be alone with scary feelings is a normal reaction to dealing with abuse. Having a therapist or counselor to talk to is one positive way not to feel so alone. Another way to find company is to join groups that have positive goals, whether it's a singing group, or people that help older people with chores, a school club, or a church group.

The energy you'll have to put into learning who to trust and how to make real friends is worth the effort. Make it a goal for yourself and get any help you need to make it work. Think about whether the person treats you and other people well, cares about what's best for you, and cares about himself or herself. You can do and enjoy all the positive things that kids your age do.

so let's remember ...

☼ Feeling good about yourself involves many things, including your self-esteem, your relationships, and the choices you make in life.

☼ Self-talk can raise or lower your self-esteem.

☼ You can change negative self-talk into positive self-talk.

☼ You have both the right and the ability to get back on the road *you choose.*

helpful things to do

journal time

1. Think of as many positive, true self-talk messages as you can, and list them.

_____

_____

_____

_____

_____

Make a plan for how these messages will become a regular part of your life. Where will you post them? When will you say them to yourself? Write down your plan. Then use it.

_____

_____

_____

_____

_____

When do you feel best about yourself? Write about a time when you felt proud of yourself.

_____

_____

_____

_____

_____

2.

What three things are you good at? What three things do you think you *might* be good at? Write them down.

_____

_____

_____

_____

_____

List at least three things (or more) you have never tried to do before, but you'd like to try.

_____

_____

_____

_____

_____

_____

_____

_____

Write about something you tried and weren't good or successful at. What skills did it take? What do you remember most about it? What did you learn from the experience?

_____

_____

_____

_____

_____

_____

_____

_____

3.

Did any of your relationships with friends or family members (not including the abuser) change after the abuse? Write about how they changed. Do you see them more or less? Do you do different things with them now than before? How have your feelings about them changed?

_____

_____

_____

_____

_____

_____

List the friends or family members (not including the abuser) you'd like to be close to but that you're having a hard time trusting.

_____

_____

_____

_____

_____

_____

Write about what makes a person trustworthy. Do you think you're trustworthy? Why?

_____

_____

_____

_____

_____

_____

your space

your space

Chapter 6

What About the Rest of My Life: Relationships

You may have a lot of questions about how sexual abuse will affect different parts of your life. In this chapter, we'll try to look at the things you may be dealing with today because of the abuse, and also what it might mean to you tomorrow, next year, or later on in your life.

with yourself

As you read in the last chapter, abuse changes relationships, including your relationship with yourself. You read about your inside self in Chapter 5, but you also have an outside self—your body—and your relationship with it may feel different since the abuse.

body image

Body image has to do with how you feel about your physical self. Do you like being inside your skin? Do you like how you look when you see yourself in a mirror? When you think about your body do you get a good feeling?

Many girls and women don't feel good about their bodies, even if they weren't sexually abused. TV and magazines keep selling the message that there is only one way to be pretty and that being pretty is the only thing that counts. The truth is that people naturally come in all shapes and sizes, and much of it has to do with our parents and their parents. You can be beautiful and like your body for other things than being "pretty."

Think back to the time before you were molested. How did your body feel? Did you enjoy your body then? You might have enjoyed watching it grow taller, or that you could sing, play music, or dance (even by yourself in your room). Maybe you enjoyed your body because you were strong or flexible and you could run fast or bend all over. You can still do and enjoy all those things about your body.

If you didn't enjoy your body before you were molested, it may be harder to enjoy your body now. And sexual abuse leaves a lot of girls feeling even worse about their bodies. Here are some of the reasons we've heard from girls who felt bad about their bodies:

I should have been able to fight him off.

I feel dirty.

I wish it didn't feel good when she touched me.

If I didn't look good, he wouldn't have been sexual with me.

If I wasn't so ugly I'd have had a boyfriend and my uncle wouldn't have said he was doing me a favor by having sex with me.

I hate my body because it got abused.

Have you thought anything like this recently? All of these ideas mean that sexual abuse has gotten connected to your body image. The first step to changing your body image is to notice these kind of messages.

Begin to notice girls and women who look nice to you. Look in other places than just at magazines and television. Magazines and TV show only images of beauty that are unrealistic and use special clothing, make-up, lighting, and camera work to create an image. In most magazines and TV shows you see only women who look like fashion models. They encourage us to only consider a limited idea of beauty, just one kind of body type and appearance.

Look at women of different ages, different skin colors, different heights and sizes. Notice how many different ways people can show beauty. You may start to notice that beauty really comes from inside. People who are happy, who love what they are doing, and who are involved in the world are often wonderful to look at and be with.

If you feel bad about your body, you can change to feeling better and then to feeling good! Make sure to look at the helpful things to do at the end of this chapter.

feeling okay about your sexuality

All of us want to feel okay about ourselves sexually. Most of us had questions and felt confused when we were trying to figure out what our sexuality was all about. Sexual abuse can make it even more confusing. In the list below are some questions we've heard from girls who were sexually abused and answers we would give.

When the time comes that I choose to have a sexual relationship with someone, will that person be able to tell I was sexually abused?

No, not unless you decide to tell your chosen partner. If you have questions about how the abuse has affected your body, a medical doctor or a nurse practitioner is a good person to talk to. Also, when you choose to be sexually active, talk to a doctor or nurse practitioner about protecting yourself from sexually transmitted diseases (like HIV) and preventing pregnancy.

If the person who abused me was a woman, does that make me a lesbian?

(Other words for this: gay, homosexual, queer.
Mean words you may hear: dyke, lezzie, fag or faggot.)

No. Being sexually abused by another girl or by a woman does not mean you were already homosexual (someone who is sexually attracted to people of their own sex), and it does not make you one afterward. Most researchers believe that people's sexual orientation (whether they are attracted to men, women, or both) is already there when we are born.

If a girl has homosexual or heterosexual (attracted to the opposite sex) *feelings, does that mean she deserved the abuse?*

Of course not! Having sexual feelings is normal, sometimes wonderful, and never means that you deserved to be abused. No one deserves to be sexually abused. People are not more or less valuable because of being attracted to one sex or the other. People who think gays and lesbians deserve to be badly treated are usually afraid of others who are different from them. Your sexual feelings are yours to explore, and no one should take advantage of them to abuse you.

Is it normal to masturbate (touch yourself sexually for your own pleasure) *and have fantasies about sex?*

Yes. For many kids, masturbation and sexual fantasies are a natural part of learning about and enjoying their own sexuality. If your fantasies during masturbation are connected to the abuse or make you feel scared, worried, guilty, or angry, it may mean that sex and abuse are still connected for you (the abuser's fault, not yours). You'll need help getting those two ideas unconnected so you can experience more positive feelings about your sexuality.

Will I ever be able to have a good sexual relationship?

YES!

The words "sexual" and "abuse" are strange words to have to put together. "Sexual" or "sex" is something normal and good, and "abuse" is not good at all. Every person has sexual feelings, thoughts and experiences. Because you were abused in a sexual way, sometimes your normal sexual feelings may remind you about the abuse. You may wonder if the abuse will happen again because you feel sexual. If this happens to you, it means that the two ideas "sex" and "abuse" are connected for you in a way that is hurting you.

Here are some ideas about beginning to DISconnect "sexual" and "abuse." Think of a time when you felt sexual feelings in your body and it wasn't about remembering being sexually abused. Look at the person you felt sexual about. Is there something about the person that reminds you about sexual abuse? Is he or she pushy? Is he or she mean? Is he or she trying to talk you into something sexual that you aren't sure you want to do? If any of your answers to these questions is "yes," maybe the "sexual" idea and the "abuse" idea are occurring together because this is true! No one has any right to force, convince, bribe, or push you sexually. NO ONE. Not your boyfriend, not your girlfriend, not your family. Being sexual is only good if *you* want to be and the other person does too, period. Not want it some and don't want it some. Trust your inner warning bell.

Honest, good sex is not about power. It's about being old enough and mature enough to share warm, wonderful, exciting feelings with someone you care about and who cares about you. In a relationship like this, neither partner uses power over the other to get what he or she wants. Both people have a say, and both people's say counts. In a good, equal relationship, no one says, "Have sex with me or else I won't go out with you." When sex is not about power, no one says, "If you really love me, prove it by having sex with me."

So, what if you *want* to hug and kiss someone you're attracted to? You look really closely and see that the person is very nice and not pushy, but you still feel all the same feelings you did with the abuse (sicky-scared inside, worried, mad, dizzy, "funny"). Each person feels differently. This is a good time for you to talk to a very safe, helping person—if you are in therapy, your therapist can help with this. It would probably be a tough one to figure out without help.

with your family

Sexual abuse always leads to a family crisis. Your family may have a little crisis or a big crisis, depending on a lot of things you have *no* control over. If the sexual abuser was someone outside the family, your family will be shocked but can probably deal with the crisis a little more easily. They are more likely to be mad at the right person—the abuser. They may understand that you're very upset and confused inside. They can know that it may take time, but this confused, scared, mad period in your life can be helped.

When a family member is the abuser, the family usually is more mixed up. The family may even try to keep the abuse a secret. Families *cannot* solve this problem on their own. That's why there are laws that require special people outside the family to help the family with its crisis. We know that help ordered by the courts often doesn't feel comfortable. But it is better than keeping the abuse a family secret. Remember, unless someone outside the family learns about the abuse, the abuse will NOT stop. As long as the abuse continues, the girl is being hurt; and the longer it goes on, the more she's hurt. No one can begin to heal until the abuse stops.

We hope that in the future you and your family can be proud that you took care of something very sad and troubling in your family by telling about the abuse. People can often grow very close when they work on something difficult together. Your family may even find new ways to talk about problems and to face them.

when your family won't or can't help

Sometimes finding out about sexual abuse doesn't lead to better ways of being a family. Sometimes (especially when the person who abused you is a member of your family) people refuse to face the truth.

Sometimes family members are so much in denial that they totally refuse to let anyone help at all. They even refuse to keep their children safe. Sometimes the family has more and more problems and there is a divorce. This is NEVER your fault. It's the job of adults to work out their own problems. Sometimes they can't or don't or won't do the work. Other times, you might wish there *would* be a divorce so that the person who has abused you would be out of your life. And sometimes that doesn't happen either, so the kids have to go live with another family (relatives or a foster family) that is safer. Sometimes kids who are in foster care go home later on. Some kids stay in their foster families. If you are growing up in a new family, we hope you find a good life there, as many kids do. If you are in foster care and you are unhappy with the foster family, tell your social worker. She may be able to help with what's going on, and if necessary, find you a new family.

Remember, even if your family won't get help and face the truth, YOU CAN GET HELP.

at school

Probably no one at school knows that you were sexually abused unless you told them. If you haven't, you may *want* someone to know so they can help out. It may be good to have someone at school that you can talk to, like a school counselor or your teacher.

It's probably not a good idea to tell other kids until you think carefully about it and maybe talk with a trusted adult. We want you to be *sure* it's a good idea. Kids can get scared about sexual abuse just like adults. And kids can also be very curious about sexual things, but not always grown up enough to understand or know how to help. This part of your life should only be shared with people who can keep it private. Besides, sexual abuse is only one part of your life. It is a part that will likely get less and less important as time goes on. School is a place to learn and make friends. If school is not a good place for you now, you can turn that around if you want. If school is a good place for you, it can keep going well.

with other friends

Unless you decide to tell them, your friends probably won't know you've been sexually abused. Just like at school, you may feel mixed up about what you want people around you to know. A lot of time you may want no one to know, and other times you may wish you had someone your own age to talk to. It's natural to want to share and talk about important things with a friend. Do you have a very trusted friend, someone who has gone through a lot together with you and who you've known a long time? If so, she or he might be someone to talk with about what has happened.

It's possible that there is a group in your area where girls your age who have been sexually abused get together and talk. This can be helpful and comforting. If you are interested, tell your caseworker, therapist, parent or another adult who is helping you. They may be able to help you find a group like this.

Sometimes we know that you just want to have fun and enjoy yourself and your friends without thinking about sexual abuse. We know that you can do and enjoy all the things that you want to do and that being sexually abused does not have to always get in the way.

If you find that making friends and having fun is hard to do, it's important to get help. Even though a terrible thing has happened to you, you can still be a good friend. People who have been through very difficult times can be the best kind of friends when they choose to use their hard experiences to become more caring and understanding.

with social services

The law says that anyone who is under age 18 and was sexually abused must be referred to an agency that protects children and teens. If you are involved with an agency like this, you probably have a social worker or caseworker. This person may have a lot to do with your life. The caseworker may contact people who know you, have a lot of recommendations to help your family, and go with you to court, if necessary.

Your relationship with your caseworker is important. Try to be open with him or her about what you want and what you don't want. She (or he) may not be able to do what you want, but maybe she can. He (or she) can't do something you want him to unless he knows about it.

During this time you may notice that with some of the decisions you have to make, there seems to be no good choice at all. That's because none of the choices are something you really want. A good social worker will help you make these very hard decisions. It is important that you have a say in what happens. Choosing the one that feels "least bad" is a way to have *some* control in your life. If sexual abuse has been in your life for a while, it may feel very different to have a choice. At first it may seem weird, but in time you'll experience that having a say in your life feels good. You don't have to be happy about hard choices, but it is good to know your ideas count.

with courts

We won't talk a lot about court because court is so different in every state. We will say that if you have to go to court, then you deserve a lot of help. You need to talk with the lawyers and have time to ask plenty of questions. The lawyers or social workers should tell you what to expect, what the other lawyers will probably say, and what they think you'll need to talk about. They should explain about the law, what laws were broken and what you can do to help yourself. You should also have a chance to go inside the courtroom before the court date so you can see what it looks like. Even if the lawyer or caseworker doesn't offer to show you the courtroom, remember that you can ask them to.

Going to court is never fun, but it can be positive. Sometimes girls feel that the chance to tell their story really helped. Sometimes telling the court can stop the abuser from abusing someone else in the future. These are very good reasons to do something that is hard.

We are sorry to say that sometimes the abuser is found not guilty. This does not mean you were wrong to tell or that the judge did not believe you. Courts need certain facts that can be proved. This idea of proof is easy in bank robberies, for instance. You may have witnesses, fingerprints, and even a video-tape that recorded the whole thing! Sexual abuse is almost the opposite. If there were other people there, they may be too scared, or too mean, or too guilty to say so. There are no fingerprints. That's why sexual abuse can be hard to prove and why people who are sexually abusive may not be found guilty. NOT because it didn't happen. Everyone may even know it happened in their minds, but without legal kinds of proof, the judge cannot find someone guilty.

with the abuser

Some girls have contact with the person who abused them, while some may never have or want contact. Some girls want to have contact with the abuser and some don't. It's a very personal decision that depends on many things.

example

Crystal hasn't seen her dad since she told about him abusing her. She is embarrassed and afraid to tell anyone how much she misses him. It's been three months since he last molested her, and it seems almost like it was a dream. She has to testify in court soon and she's feeling awful. She can't concentrate in school. She feels sick a lot and she isn't sleeping very well. Her teacher noticed and called her mom. Her mom called the social worker, who began to ask more questions about Crystal's feelings. She didn't mean to tell but the whole thing just started to spill out ... that she was sorry she told about her dad, how much she wished it had never happened, and that she felt like all the trouble was her fault.

Crystal was surprised and relieved when Astrid, her caseworker, seemed to understand completely. They talked for quite a while about how much she missed her dad. Then Crystal remembered again about how awful the abuse was and how much she REALLY hated it. She remembered how mad she is that her dad says that the abuse is just a story she's making up to get attention and that it never happened. She realized she was mad at him because it was his fault that she was missing him. She let the social worker help her with all of her feelings and they made a safety plan for court (including where she would look so she didn't have to look at her dad at all).

Sometimes you can't avoid seeing the person who abused you because he or she goes to your school or lives in your neighborhood. Sometimes when the abuser is a parent, a court may order you to visit him or her. If this is true for you, then you will need to have a plan to help you not feel too scared.

Depending on your school situation, the principal, a guidance counselor, or your teacher may be able to help prevent the abuser from being around you or doing anything scary and intimidating. They might change the abuser's lunch time or classroom, for example. You might need to be prepared for the abuser to start nasty rumors about you, and there's not much that anyone can do about that, except keep your head up and remember that you didn't do anything wrong. A trusted helper at school can work with you on creating and keeping up a special safety plan.

If the abuser lives in your neighborhood, again, you need a special plan to help you feel and be safe. Sometimes your parents can help you with this plan, and sometimes you'll need to find ways to deal with it yourself. Spend some time thinking about how you can be safe. Remember that safety means both safety inside yourself as well as outside, what you can do as well as what others can do to help.

example

Kashone was molested by Bruce, an older boy who went to a different school. She never expected to see him again. A couple of months after she told about the abuse, she went to a party at a friend of a friend's house, and Bruce walked through the door! She froze ... but then she reminded herself that there were *lots* of people around. She decided she was safe, and because she already knew Bruce wasn't safe to be around, he wouldn't be able to surprise her like he had before. Next she called her mom right away and asked her to come and get her. She asked her friends Jeannie and Dara to stay with her until her mom arrived. There was one bad moment when Kashone saw Bruce looking over in her direction. She took a deep breath and looked right back at him, thinking, "YOU CAN'T HURT ME AGAIN!" Then she turned and walked away. He didn't follow. Kashone and her mom talked a lot about how well she had handled the situation.

Each person's situation is different. You can't always tell what's going to happen when you see the person who abused you. Remember: you have a right to protect yourself and to have help. If someone you're with sends you the message, "It's okay," and *you* don't feel okay, remember that *your* feelings are your guide to how you want to act. If the person who abused you sends the message, "When will you trust me again?" remember that it is *your* decision. "When you've earned my trust by not ignoring my feelings" might be one answer. Sometimes "never" might be the answer. You may like the person, but not trust him or her.

example

Caitlyn's dad molested her when she was six years old. He went to jail, and then got out. When she was eight, he began court-ordered visitation. They would see each other every two weeks at her grandma's house, her dad's mom's. After a while, Caitlyn looked forward to the visits because he always brought a present, he was really happy to see her, and she missed him. But this last time, he asked her to sit on his lap, and she felt icky inside. She said, "I don't want to, I like sitting in my *own* chair, Dad." When Caitlyn got home, she told her mom about it and about her icky feelings. Her mom said, "You did great! You never have to sit in his lap if you don't want to. I'll talk to him and to Grandma, and we'll set some limits, okay? I want Grandma to always back you up if you don't want to do something with him." Caitlyn had started writing in her journal, and her mom said maybe she could write down things like this that happened during her visits, so she could keep track of whether things changed.

In any situation, kids need coping tools inside themselves to help them feel strong and powerful when they see the person who abused them. They need inner ways of reminding themselves that, first, they didn't do anything wrong, and second, the situation is not the same. You and your helpers have worked to make sure that the abuser does not have the same power over you or the same opportunity to use it as before.

People who sexually abuse children often say they have changed. We know that, especially for an adult abuser, it takes a long time to change from wanting to sexually abuse to not wanting to sexually abuse. It takes many years and lots of hard work. If your abuser says he or she has changed, maybe it's true, and maybe it's just the abuser's wishful thinking. We feel that you should be very careful with your feelings and your body. Even when you like this person, it makes sense to be very careful with an abuser who has hurt you in the past. This relationship is very complicated. You may remember very caring times you had with him or her. The person may have been very kind in some ways. But if he or she still has the inner desire to be sexual with you, it can be hard to protect yourself. It takes a special kind of inner power to be able to be close to an abuser AND protect yourself from any sneaky way he or she may try to be sexual. Remember, any person who should know better and behaves in a sexual way with a kid has a BIG problem. It will take that person a long time to change deep down inside where it counts.

with the world

Most things about being sexually abused are bad, and you may always feel bad or sad about it even when you learn to feel good about yourself. But some of the results of your sexual abuse may surprise you. You see, *everyone* has some bad experiences in their lives. On TV you've seen people experience terrible things—like tornadoes, or going to jail unfairly, or being treated badly because of the color of their skin, or having a serious birth defect. Some people become very bitter and angry about these things. But MANY people make good use of these bad experiences. They learn they had strengths they didn't know they had. They learn about themselves, about what went wrong and about ways to protect themselves in the future.

There are many strengths that people who have healed from sexual abuse may find about themselves. They know that children deserve special care and can teach their own children to be both careful and strong in the world. They can be open to other children and people who need care and attention. They can develop good "radar" or intuition about people.

It's important to look closely at your intuition or "radar" feelings. Your inner voice is often trying to tell you information about the world. Haven't you heard someone say "I *knew* I shouldn't have..." or "I just had a feeling..."? They were talking about their "radar" feelings. No one's intuition is perfect. People who have been sexually abused may go through a time when they feel like almost everyone might be mean or abusive. If you feel that way, you probably have scared feelings deep inside that you need to talk about with someone you can trust. The opposite sometimes happens, too—some people who have been abused may be totally trusting of everyone. They are probably not using their intuition, and that makes them less safe.

Trusting your intuition means paying attention to feeling "unsure" about a person or an action. Let's say you meet a person who is always smiling and friendly, but inside you feel tense when you're with him—or her. That may be your radar picking up information. Maybe you are picking up that this person feels too "pushy" or that he or she feels mad underneath. Your feelings may or may not be right, but they are worth noticing. You may want to spend more time getting to know the person or watching how he or she acts. You may decide you don't want to be around that person, or you may find out later that he or she was just as nervous as you were meeting someone new. Radar can't protect anyone all the time, but it can be a part of you that gives you good information.

Many people who have been sexually abused have a deep understanding about certain truths. They really *know* that nice, innocent, good people get hurt. They know that people get hurt, and it's not their fault. They can become strong people who stand up for truth and goodness in the world. They have the power and courage to fight against cruelty. We hope you find some positive things about yourself and your strengths along your road to healing. We know that everyone has the power to make this happen.

so let's remember ...

☼ Relationships with yourself, family members, friends, at school and in the world can get a little complicated after abuse. But with some coping tools, you can handle it.

☼ Every person has her own kind of beauty, and self-esteem means more than being "pretty" on the outside.

☼ It's normal to feel confused about sexual feelings, even for kids who weren't sexually abused. It's possible, but not easy, to separate sexual feelings from feelings about abuse.

☼ When feelings about sexual abuse come up, it's a good idea to ask yourself, "Why am I thinking about this now?" Maybe you are feeling emotionally close to someone; maybe someone is scaring you; or maybe more feelings are coming up because you are reading this book.

☼ Paying attention to your intuition about people and situations can help keep you safe.

☼ People who have experienced sexual abuse can grow up to be kind, courageous, tough, and smart. That's because all people can grow from hard times in their lives.

helpful things to do

imagery time

Some people have an inside place where they get feelings about other people or situations. They call this their "radar." What do you think about the idea of radar? Do you think you have any radar senses inside you? What would it look like? How do you think you can check it out to see if it is trustworthy? Have you had inside feelings that you know have been true? Write about your radar and how you found out whether it was true.

_____

_____

_____

_____

_____

_____

_____

journal time

1. What is the most helpful thing that a family member has done for you since the abuse? A friend? A teacher or classmate? What do you wish a family member, a friend, a teacher, or a classmate would do to help you? How might you help make that happen?

_____

_____

_____

_____

_____

_____

2.

Draw a picture of your body in your journal or on this page. Don't worry about how good the drawing is—an outline or a stick figure will work fine.

Mark the areas of your body with different colors. Pick one color for parts that you like. Pick a second color for parts that are okay. Pick a third color for parts you don't like.

Take a look at your picture. What do you notice? How much of each color is there? If you did this drawing five years ago, how would be different? How do you think it will be different when you are 21? How would you like to be different?

Pick a part of your body either that you like or that you think is okay. Decide on something you can do to notice that part of you more, take good care of it, and help it feel good or look nice or both!

examples

Miranda noticed that on her picture she had colored her legs purple (her favorite color). She thought about her legs and realized that she liked them because they were a really strong part of her. She could run fast and race up the stairs at school quickly and without even breathing hard. She thought about how she could take good care of them. First she noticed her skin was dry, so she put some lotion on them. Then she put on her softest socks and her most comfortable sneakers. Finally, she went out and walked all around her block so her legs would stay loose, limber and ready to go.

Ming had colored her hands blue for okay. She liked how her nails looked since she had stopped biting them and how strong her hands were from piano practice. She loved the way her rings looked on her hands when she wasn't practicing. She decided to buff her nails shiny and got herself a manicure kit so she could keep her nails short without biting them.

Write down why you like some part of your body and something nice you can do for that part.

_____

_____

_____

_____

_____

Now try the same thing with a part of your body you don't like much. Think of positive things about it, or ways you can relate to it differently. Think of how you can change your negative feelings to positive ones. See whether there is any negative self-talk going on about that part of your body. Catch those thoughts and replace them with positive ones. If you don't like a part of your body because it is weak, think about how you can strengthen it. Write about that part of your body.

_____

_____

_____

_____

_____

_____

Look at pictures in magazines and books and snapshots of people you know. Find pictures of people you admire for what they do in the world. When you find people pictures that make you feel good, put them on your bulletin board or in your notebook or journal for a few weeks. Find faces that you won't see all over the place, new and different faces. Surprise your friends with pictures of people they've never seen, and tell them something about the person that they didn't know before.

3.

Who can you talk to about sexual feelings? Write down what you'd like to say.

_____

_____

_____

_____

_____

_____

_____

_____

_____

_____

_____

_____

_____

4.

What do you think you'll feel if you meet the person who abused you again? What would you like to do, or how would you like to act? What inside message would you need to tell yourself to help you feel strong? If you already have seen the abuser, write about what you felt, what you did or what you wish you could have done, and what your inside message was.

_____

_____

_____

_____

_____

_____

_____

_____

5.

Do you know anyone who had a really bad experience and learned something or found that something good came out of it? Write about that person.

example

A friend of ours named Rachel had a dog she really loved when she was six years old. She had picked out the puppy, named him Ralph, cared for him, taught him tricks, and loved him. Ralph even slept on her bed. When she was ten she accidentally let Ralph out the door before she could get his leash on, and he got hit by a car. When Ralph died, Rachel was heartbroken and she felt so guilty. No one in her family blamed her because they knew it was an accident and that she never would hurt Ralph on purpose. It was a terrible way to learn to be more careful, but she did just that. She also decided to become a good animal healer and got good grades in school. She is now a veterinarian.

If you don't know any examples, ask people around you if they have ever learned something from a sad or bad experience.

_____
_____
_____
_____
_____
_____
_____
_____
_____
_____

What things have you learned so far from your experience of sexual abuse? Write about that and talk about it with a trusted person.

_____
_____
_____
_____
_____

your space

your space

Chapter 7

Therapy

There are lots of professional people who are therapists. Therapists can be trained as social workers, counselors, psychologists, nurses and psychiatrists. Therapists can be men or women. But therapists all have the same job: to help you talk about what happened and what is happening to you so you can feel better.

why do I need a therapist to talk to?

We know that you may have been managing pretty well without a therapist for talking about being sexually abused. However, you probably have felt very alone with your feelings about it. Sexual abuse causes so many feelings—different, often confusing and even disagreeing with each other. It often takes special help to work them out. It's extremely hard for people who've been sexually abused to get their feelings sorted out all by themselves.

why can't I just talk to my friends?

It's great that you have friends to talk to. You may even have a friend who has had similar things happen in her or his life. She or he will be an especially important person right now. However, talking with a therapist is different from talking it out with a friend. A good therapist has talked with many girls and boys who've been abused. Your therapist should make therapy private and confidential (just between the two of you) in order to keep your ideas safe. There's a difference between privacy and secrecy: keeping secrets can be dangerous—that's how the abuser tried not to be caught.

Privacy, or keeping something confidential (say CON fih DEN shul), refers to something that's just yours, not because it's bad, but because it's nobody else's business. Information about the person or people who abused you is not confidential. Your therapist may tell your social worker information about them so they can't hurt you or anyone else again. Another thing that your therapist may need to share with someone else is when you are doing something dangerous to yourself or to another person. Your therapist's first concern is making sure you are safe. If you have other questions about therapy and privacy, be sure to ask your therapist.

A word of advice about talking to friends. A lot of people are pretty ignorant about sexual abuse. They might think it's funny or that it's something to gossip about. They may just not understand at all. This can be surprising and hurtful when you've thought about that person as a friend. When you choose people to talk to, you want to be as sure as you can to choose helpful, safe people.

but I'd rather not talk about it at all

That's how you may have coped for a long time, so no wonder you think that's the best way to keep handling it. In fact, that's the way a lot of girls get through this: "Don't think about it...don't talk about it!" Before, the best way you knew how to handle it was to keep it a secret. But, remember it's not a secret anymore. Because you may have never really talked about it, the relief you might feel by letting it out with someone (like a therapist) who understands it is a new experience.

I feel too embarrassed

Nothing you say about anyone—your mom, your dad, or the person who abused you (they may be the same person)—can surprise, shock, or hurt your therapist. That's the good thing about a therapist. She isn't involved with anyone or anything in your life except you. Her job is to help you put the abuse in an "easier-to-deal-with" place in your life and learn new coping tools.

what if I get really upset?

The purpose of therapy is to make a safe place for you to express any and all of your feelings. Safety means ALL of your feelings are okay. If you are like most girls, you may notice that many more feelings are coming out of you than you knew were inside. Again—a therapist will be expecting this—it's perfectly normal. This is the first time you could let it all out. It may feel like a lot, but remember—you've been holding your feelings inside a long time.

what therapy should feel like

Therapy and your therapist should feel safe. But feeling safe is not always the same as feeling *comfortable*. You might feel uncomfortable sometimes, or even dread going to therapy because it is so hard, but even then, you will be safe. You should feel that your therapist is *really* listening and paying attention to you. It's best if she asks questions about your life, including things at school and at home, to understand how sexual abuse has affected you. Right now, you probably don't know all the ways it has become part of your life.

After a short time, therapy will probably be a place you look forward to going to. It's good to know you can get things out and say anything. It's okay to get mad or sad or embarrassed with your therapist. People sometimes get mad at therapists because they can't make bad things go away and horrible feelings stop quickly. But they can't. Feeling better usually takes time and hard work.

what will I do in therapy?

Therapy can happen in lots of different ways. While you may feel too old to color or play, it's very common even for adults to do those things in therapy. Don't be surprised if your therapist brings out crayons, clay, or paint. You may just talk together or sometimes you might talk and do something else at the same time. You may even feel like it's easier to express a particular feeling through art or play.

Eventually, other people may become a part of

your therapy. It may be a good idea to ask members of your family to come in and talk. This should happen only when you feel ready. The therapist's job is to help you make your life better and often it requires other people's help.

ways to help your therapist

People who have been sexually abused help themselves in some special ways. As we have mentioned, one way is to try to forget about being abused. Many people, even while being abused, find a way to make it feel like it isn't happening at all or it isn't happening to them. They take themselves out of their situation in a special imaginary way that feels totally real. Remember, therapists call this dissociation.

We started to talk about dissociation in previous chapters when we talked about feeling "spaced out." Dissociation happens lots of different ways. Here are some examples. Have you had any of these experiences?

You know it happened, but don't know what you did.
Kayla remembers that her big brother came into her room and made her be quiet. She was really scared. But then her memory gets very fuzzy. Even when Kayla tries to remember what happened next, she can't.

You know it happened, but don't know what you felt.
Danielle's friend James seemed so nice and fun to be with, and she was happy he wanted to spend time with her. Danielle remembers the day in the woods when James started acting funny, grabbed her, pushed her down, and pulled off her clothes. She remembers when he stopped and then walked her home. But when people ask her how she felt, she has no idea. Danielle knows that if this happened to someone else she would feel angry and scared for them. But when she thinks about it happening to her, she feels nothing or kind of numb.

You know it happened, but don't know what your body felt.
Cindy remembers her babysitter Derek putting her hand on his penis and she remembers feeling first curious and then scared. The weird thing was she couldn't feel anything in her hand. Later, when Derek tried to push his fingers inside Cindy's vagina, she couldn't feel that either. In fact, Cindy felt like she had left her body and was watching what was happening to her from far away.

You have no memory of anything.

Tina's family remembers what happened because her mom walked in while her aunt was lying next to her and both of them were undressed and hugging. When Tina's mom talks about it, Tina gets a strange feeling in her body, but she doesn't remember anything about her aunt doing anything like that.

All of these examples are some of the ways that people dissociate, but it happens in lots of other ways too. Dissociation is a way of building walls around abuse. Just like different people build different fences or walls around their yards, the walls people build with dissociation come out differently. No two people do it exactly the same way.

The problem with dissociation is that it helps very well while the abuse is happening, but it is not a good permanent way to help inside. Ideas that are "put away" through dissociation have a way of "leaking out." It's confusing to feel things that just don't make sense logically. For example, if the person who sexually abused you wore a green shirt and you dissociated everything about the abuse, you still might feel weird whenever you see the color green. So let's go back to the idea of how to help your therapist. Tell her or him about any confusing ideas, feelings and experiences.

Remembering what happened to you can come about in different ways. It can happen in dreams, in tiny feelings, or quick pictures in your mind. These are called "flashbacks" and they can be scary and confusing. A therapist acts like a good detective, and together you can make sense out of things that at first make no sense at all. Once you remember the *real* reason you are scared or confused or numb, you won't need to have these strange feelings. We believe that everything you experience can make sense eventually. A therapist is the right person to help you figure things out.

what if I hate it?

If you feel like you hate therapy, those feelings are important to pay attention to. The next question to ask yourself is—*why* do I hate it? You might be getting the message from other people that therapy is a bad thing and that going to therapy means you're crazy. They may say that it's too expensive or that it's hard to keep taking you there. They may hint or even say right out very hurtful things—like you are just faking feeling bad or that your feeling bad is hurting them. If you see the person who abused you, he or she may suggest these things.

If anyone is sending you these messages, talk with your therapist about it. We know this is hard, but one way is to ask her to read this part of the book. Then your therapist can help you figure out a way to get the person to stop, maybe by helping the person understand more about what's going on.

Another reason that you might hate therapy is that you may not like your therapist. Maybe you feel she's not listening to you. Maybe you're mad about something he said. What we said about *all* of your feelings being important is true here too. Feelings about your therapist are very important. If you don't like or even hate your therapist, tell someone. It's best to tell your therapist, but if that's too hard, tell someone else. Maybe your social worker or your parents. Things can change, but they change easiest when people know there is a problem.

Another reason you may hate therapy or hate your therapist is that you're not sure you can trust her or him. You may wonder if the questions are meant to make you feel sad or mad. She (or he) will ask questions (if she really is trying to help) about very hard, sad parts of your life. It's okay to be mad at her, because she can take it and not get mad back. It's okay to take your time and watch and listen, and then decide if she or he is okay.

Even the best therapy sometimes feels scary. If you hate therapy because you feel scared, try to figure out what is scaring you. Some kids get scared because of being in a small room with an adult with the door closed. Some kids get scared because when they feel the feelings about the abuse, they feel scared. Some therapists give pats on the shoulder or encouraging hugs, and those may feel scary. Try to figure out what's scary so you can tell your therapist and you can work out some changes together. If you can't figure out what's scary, tell your therapist that you're feeling scared so she or he can help you figure out why.

If you are scared because the therapist has touched you sexually or hit you, it's important that you know that a therapist should NEVER sexually touch or hit a kid. These things are abusive and are NEVER part of good therapy. Tell someone about it, your parent or guardian, your case worker, a guidance counselor or a teacher. Tell someone who will help you find a therapist who understands and respects you.

so what's important here?

We think therapy is a good idea and that every sexually abused person should have a chance to talk to a therapist. Therapy needs to be safe; you need to feel that you can say anything. You also need to feel that it is helping—if it isn't, you need to tell your therapist or someone else who can help.

We wish we could say that therapy is easy and always works quickly. That's not true. Therapy is not like magic, and even with a *great* therapist, therapy takes work. But over time, therapy can help you make your life easier and happier and safer.

therapy in your future

Therapy is often useful at one time and not at another. You may want to work hard in therapy and feel better and then stop therapy for a while. Later on you may go back and do some more work and then stop. Think of therapy as a check-up with a safe guide. As you grow and change, new things may happen that you want to talk about. This is normal.

so let's remember ...

☼ The best way to help your therapist help you is to talk about your true feelings, no matter what they are.

☼ EVERYONE has ideas, feelings and behavior that bother them sometimes.

☼ Your therapist has heard very similar things from other kids. She won't think you are weird or strange.

helpful things to do

imagery time

Everyone needs a safe place in life. Lots of people have inside safe places as well as outside safe places. Imagine the safest place you can. Some people take "safe place" ideas from books or memories or make it up in their own minds. Make it just the way you want. Put all of your favorite things in there. Practice going to the safe place inside just before you go to sleep at night. Check in a few times during the day, just so you know it's there. If it feels like it has faded, just add to it. You may want two inside safe places. Everyone has the right to have a feeling of inside safety and to make their safe place better and better.

journal time

Write down a description of your safe place.

example

Laverne was trying to make a safe place in her mind and she couldn't! It never felt quite right. She thought a long time about what it would *really* take to feel safe. She decided that if her safe place were on an island, it would be safe enough. Her inside safe place became a beautiful island in the Pacific where it was always warm. There were specially trained sharks and whales to protect her all around the island.

_____

_____

_____

_____

_____

_____

_____

Have you had a flashback? Did you know what it was? Write down your experience.

example

Whenever Rosie tried to fall asleep in her bed where she had been abused, she began to feel very tense and her body felt very tight. She could feel her heart beat faster. It was very hard to fall asleep and she felt tired all the time.

_____

_____

_____

_____

_____

_____

If you've told another person about a flashback, write down how you and she figured out how to help.

example

Rosie talked to her mom about her fears about her room. She and her mom rearranged her furniture so the room felt different. Before she went to sleep, Rosie had her mom remind her that no one unsafe was in the house. Rosie then would say to herself "I am safe and my room is safe." Rosie and her therapist started a special flashback section in her journal. In it, she wrote down all of her flashbacks and in therapy they worked on her memories. As she put all the pieces of her memories together, the flashbacks stopped on their own.

_____

_____

_____

_____

_____

_____

_____

_____

_____

If you are in therapy, write down three things you like about therapy and three things you don't like.

things I like about therapy

1. _____

_____

2. _____

_____

3. _____

_____

things I don't like about therapy

1. _____

_____

2. _____

_____

3. _____

_____

Think about whether you might want to show what you've written here to your therapist. Whether you share it or you don't, it's your choice and either way is okay.

your space

your space

In Closing: What You Need To Heal

In Chapter 1, we said we believed you were reading this book because you had made a decision. Whatever that decision was, it became a part of your own road to healing. Since we believe that everyone is unique and special, each person's road to healing will have its own curves and hills and valleys. Each person will need different things along the way, including some rest stops. Here are some of our ideas about what people need to heal. Add lots of your own.

personal power and safety skills

Sexual abuse is an adult problem, and adults need to work on stopping it. But all kids can help themselves by strengthening their personal power and safety skills. In our society, children get mixed messages about safety. Too often, adults warn kids, "Don't talk to strangers" and then insist that kids should *always* be polite to adults. And not talking to strangers doesn't help when the person who abused you was a relative or somebody you already knew. Kids need to learn their own safety skills and how to think for themselves in unexpected and possibly dangerous situations.

Girls who have been abused—sexually, physically, or emotionally—may have an even harder time learning to use their personal power and safety skills. Some things about the way you relate to yourself and others could put you at risk of further abuse. Ask yourself …

> Do I feel that other people's feelings are more important than mine?
>
> Have I learned not to trust my inner feelings and radar?
>
> Do I often feel bad about myself and believe I deserve any bad things that happen to me?
>
> Do I frequently "space out" and not be aware of what's going on around me?

So where do you start? If you've noticed yourself doing things that interfere with your being and feeling safe, talk about it with your social worker, therapist or another adult who is helping you. Ask your parents or your therapist or other trusted adult to help you learn more about safety.

You may want to take a self-defense or martial arts class (like karate, aikido, or tae kwan do). These classes teach good self-defense skills AND help you develop more awareness of yourself and more confidence in your body. You might find classes through the YMCA or the YWCA, a community center or even your local police department. Maybe a friend or a trusted adult will want to go to classes with you.

Some suggestions for building strength, body awareness, and self-confidence can be fun, as well as work. Take a dance or gymnastics class. Join a sports team—soccer, softball, or track. Go rollerblading. Find ways to have your body be strong and have fun.

a safe place

Am I safe?
Do I feel safe?
Do I know what it would feel like to be safe?
Who can I turn to if I don't feel safe?

For many girls who have been sexually abused, these are not simple questions. Some have felt unsafe for so long that it takes time, a lot of testing, and hard work to build their confidence in their ability to be and feel safe.

The question, "Am I safe?" is a good one to ask yourself throughout your road to healing. What do we mean by safe? First of all, are you still in danger of being sexually, physically, or emotionally abused? If so, you are not safe, and getting safe is what's most important.

While a big part of therapy is discovering your own strength and ability to help yourself, all kids *need* and *deserve* the help of at least one grownup to help them be safe. If you are unsure about your safety, please tell someone until you hear very clearly that they will protect you. This person should also be able to answer your questions about how they will do this. You can reread the section on "Some Ways to Find Help" in Chapter 1 for some more ideas about how to get the help you need.

Sometimes girls have felt so helpless and alone that they run away to try to get safe. If you have considered running away—please don't. It's too dangerous. Many runaways don't escape sexual abuse, they run into more of it by becoming prostitutes to get money or have a place to stay. If you are in danger and need another place to stay, find a trusted adult to help you plan the best way to get to a safer place. There might be a shelter especially for young runaways in your area.

Healing takes time and lots of energy. You probably cannot use your energy to heal if you are still using most of your energy to protect yourself. So again, *it's safety first*.

motivation

If only the road to healing had a short cut! For most people, healing takes lots of time and plenty of hard work. Motivation is the energy that keeps a person working towards something that they want. Being in the Olympics or being on the track team can motivate a person to keep training, exercising, and practicing, even when it means getting up early or jogging when it's cold and wet. Most roads have some rough and bumpy spots, including the road to healing. Sometimes it may not feel good at all.

It takes a great deal of bravery and motivation to heal. (What a relief, two things you already have!) Fortunately, the road to healing has many rewards, and it can actually be fun and exciting to learn and do things you never thought you could. Give yourself a pat on the back each time you make some progress. You deserve it.

balance

Most of us can't work hard *all* the time. It's probably better for you if you can take some breaks to relax and have fun. Working at healing doesn't mean you can't enjoy life.

Sometimes girls who have been sexually abused spend so much of their energy trying to cope with what has happened to them that they forget or never learn how to play and relax. If you think this has happened to you, talk to your therapist or other special helpers about it. If you want to, learning to have fun and discovering the things you like to do an be one of your goals of healing.

special helpers

Most people find the road to healing easier if they get the special help they need. This help can come from several places—good relationships, special books, attention to our spiritual needs (faith in God and our religious beliefs), therapy. These are just a few of the things we can mention. Take time to think about whether or not you have enough special helpers in your life. If not, tell this to someone who cares about you. Between the two of you, we bet you can get more of what you need and deserve. And remember, all of your special helpers don't have to deal with sexual abuse. A good friend can do a lot to help you feel better even if you choose not to talk about the abuse.

knowledge that you can turn your life into something positive

Remember that some of the most courageous, wise, and helpful people in the world had hurtful experiences in their childhood. They learned to take in new ideas and then find their strength and courage. We wish you well as you make your way along your own road to healing.

helpful things to do

Sometimes you read a book and it feels like, "Yup, that's just like me." Other times it feels like, "Nope, that's not me." It's good to think about how you feel—about books, about things that happen in your life, about people. Choose the three best ideas in this book. Which ideas or feelings fit you best? Write them down here.

_____

_____

_____

_____

_____

_____

What ideas do you wish we'd have written more about? Ideas you don't agree with? Write down three things you wish we'd talked about, talked more about, or that you disagreed with.

_____

_____

_____

_____

_____

_____

You may want to share this page with someone (a friend, or your therapist, or a parent) who knows you've been working with this book, so they can see what you think and how the book is and isn't like you. Remember, it's always your choice whether and with whom to share anything you write.

We care a lot about whether this book helped you. We want to make it even better. If you want to share with us what you've written on this page, make a copy and send it to Mindy Loiselle and Leslie Wright, _Shining Through_, Safer Society Press, P.O. Box 340, Brandon, VT 05733.

If you picked a title for your life like it was a movie, what would the title be? What would you like the title to be when you are 21 years old? Write them both down here.

_____

_____

_____

_____

_____

_____

_____

_____

If the titles are different, write down here or in your journal some things you can do to help make your life more like the second movie title. One thing might be, "Ask for help with my feelings when I need it."

_____

_____

_____

_____

_____

_____

_____

_____

your space

your space

your space

your space

recommended reading

You'll be able to find some of these books in a bookstore, and some in a library.

books about sexuality and growing up

A Kid's First Book About Sex by Joani Blank. Yes Press, Burlingame, California. 1993. A wonderful book about sexuality as experienced by children. Good for young children.

Changing Bodies, Changing Lives: A Book for Teens on Sex and Relationships by Ruth Bell. Random House, New York. 1988. By the author of *Our Bodies, Our Selves*. A complete reference for teens from a teenager's viewpoint. Includes sexual, emotional, and physical health care.

The Facts of Love, Living, Loving and Growing Up by Alex and Jane Comfort. Random House, New York. 1986. Written for teens and their parents. Sensitive and honest.

Changes in You for Girls and *Changes in You for Boys* by Peggy C. Siegel. Family Life Education Associates, P.O. Box 7466, Richmond, Virginia 23221. 1992. Both of these books are written by a family life educator. Clear and scientific, excellent for understanding the changes that come with puberty.

books about sexual abuse

These books are for younger children than this book is, and can be useful in healing.

A Very Touching Book by Jan Hindman. AlexAndria Associates, c/o The Hindman Foundation, 49 N.W. 1st St., Ontario, OR 97914. (Phone: 503-889-8938).

Good Hugs and Bad Hugs? How Can You Tell? by Angela R. Carl. Standard Publishing, Cincinnati, Ohio. 1984. This coloring book format covers many skills needed to keep safe. Religious orientation.

Chilly Stomach by Jeannette Carnes. Harper & Row. 1986. A beautifully illustrated picture book about a child who decides to share that her uncle is sexually molesting her.

No More Secrets for Me by Oralee Wachter. Little Brown and Company. Boston. 1983. A number of short examples of ways children are molested and ways they decide to get help.

Secret Feelings & Thoughts by Rosemary Narimanian. Philly Kids Play It Safe, 1650 Arch St. 17th Floor, Suite 1700, Philadelphia, PA 19103 (Phone: 215-686-3966). Story of a boy victimized by his brother, and his experience in therapy.

books about sexual abuse for older teens and adults

The Me Nobody Knows: A Guide for Teen Survivors by Barbara Bean and Shari Bennett. Lexington Books. 1993. A workbook for older teens about sexual abuse.

Beginning to Heal by Ellen Bass and Laura Davis. HarperCollins. 1993. You might start with this one, about deciding to heal yourself, then try their big book, *The Courage to Heal*, and Laura Davis's *The Courage to Heal Workbook*.

Adults Molested As Children: A Survivor's Manual for Women and Men, by Euan Bear with Peter Dimock. Safer Society Press, 72 pages, easy to read. Good for sharing with other people.

Family Fallout by Dorothy Beaulieu Laundry. Safer Society Press. 1991. About the problems that can happen in a family when a child who is now a grownup tells about being sexually abused.

For Guys My Age: A Book About Sexual Abuse for Young Men by Matthew Taylor. Hawthorne Center, 1847 Haggerty Road, Northville, MI 48761. 1990.

Back on Track: Boys Dealing with Sexual Abuse by Leslie Baily Wright and Mindy B. Loiselle. Safer Sociey Press. 1997. For boys age 10 and up.

videos about sexual abuse for adolescents and adults

Once Can Hurt a Lifetime: Marilyn Van Derbur. 1994. 30 minutes about the impact of sexual abuse by other teens. Your school may be able to get this or may already have a copy. One Voice, 1858 Park Road NW, Washington, DC 20010 (Phone: 202-667-1160).

A Story of Hope: Marilyn Van Derbur. 1992. This 52-minute video shows Marilyn Van Derbur (Miss America of 1958) speaking as a survivor of incest a few weeks after her story was in the newspapers. Marilyn Van Derbur, P.O. Box 61099, Denver, CO 80206.

Select Safer Society Publications

STOP! Just for Kids: For Kids with Sexual Touching Problems Adapted by Terri Allred and Gerald Burns (1997) $15.

Back on Track: Boys Dealing with Sexual Abuse by Leslie Bailey Wright & Mindy Loiselle (1997) $16.

Feeling Good Again: A Workbook for Children Aged 6 and Up Who've Been Sexually Abused by Burt Wasserman (1998). $16.

Feeling Good Again Guide for Parents and Therapists by Burt Wasserman (1998). $8.

37 to One: Living as an Integrated Multiple by Phoenix J. Hocking (1996). $12.

The Brother / Sister Hurt: Recognizing the Effects of Sibling Abuse by Vernon Wiehe, PhD (1996). $10.

SOS Help for Emotions: Managing Anxiety, Anger, and Depression by Lynn Clark(1998). From Parents Press $13.50.

SOS Help for Parents by Lynn Clark (2nd edition, 1996). From Parents Press $12.

When Children Abuse: Group Treatment Strategies for Children with Impulse Control Problems by Carolyn Cunningham and Kee MacFarlane. Incorporates and updates their well-respected previous volume *When Children Molest Children,* adding new material on medications, shame and entitlement, firesetting, and animal abuse. (1996). $28.

The Right Touch: A Read-Aloud Story to Help Prevent Child Sexual Abuse by Sandy Kleven, illustrated by Jody Bergsma. From Illumination Arts. $15.95.

From Trauma to Understanding: A Guide for Parents of Children with Sexual Behavior Problems by William D. Pithers, Alison S. Gray, Carolyn Cunningham, & Sandy Lane (1993). $5.

Adolescent Sexual Offender Assessment Packet by Alison Stickrod Gray & Randy Wallace (1992). $8.

The Relapse Prevention Workbook for Youth in Treatment by Charlene Steen (1993). $15.

Roadmaps to Recovery: A Guided Workbook for Young People in Treatment by Timothy J. Kahn (1999). $20.

Pathways: A Guided Workbook for Youth Beginning Treatment by Timothy J. Kahn (1990; revised 1992; 3rd printing). $15.

Pathways Guide for Parents of Youth Beginning Treatment by Timothy J. Kahn (1990). $10.

Tell It Like It Is: A Resource for Youth in Treatment by Alice Tallmadge with Galyn Foster (1998). $15.

Man-to-Man, When Your Partner Says NO: Pressured Sex & Date Rape by Scott Allen Johnson (1992). $7.50.

When You Don't Know Who to Call: A Consumer's Guide to Selecting Mental Health Care by Nancy Schaufele and Donna B. Kennedy (1998). $15.

Outside Looking In: When Someone You Love Is in Therapy by Patrice Moulton and Lin Harper (1999). $20.

The Secret: Art and Healing from Sexual Abuse by Francie Lyshak-Stelzer (1999). $20.

Adults Molested As Children: A Survivor's Manual for Women & Men by Euan Bear with Peter Dimock (1988; 4th printing). $12.95.

Family Fallout: A Handbook for Families of Adult Sexual Abuse Survivors by Dorothy Beaulieu Landry, M.Ed. (1991). $12.95.

Embodying Healing: Integrating Bodywork and Psychotherapy in Recovery from Childhood Sexual Abuse by Robert J. Timms, PhD, and Patrick Connors, CMT. (1992). $15.

The Safer Society Press publishes additional books, audiocassettes, and training videos related to the treatment of sexual abuse. For a catalog of our complete listings, please check the box on the order form (next page).

Book Order Form

Date:_____

Shipping Address:

All books shipped via United Parcel Services. Please include a street location for shipping as we can not ship to a Post Office box.

Name and/or Agency _____

Street Address (no P.O. Box) _____

City_____State _____Zip _____

Billing Address (*if different from shipping address*):

Address _____

City_____State _____Zip _____

Daytime Phone (_____)_____ P.O. #_____

Visa or MasterCard # _____ Exp. Date _____

Signature (*FOR CREDIT CARD ORDER*) _____

❏ Do not add me to your mailing list.

Qty	Title	Unit Price	Total Cost

Subtotal	
VT Residents add sales tax	
Shipping (see below)	
Total	

All orders must be prepaid.

Make checks payable to:
SAFER SOCIETY PRESS.

All prices subject to change without notice. No Returns.

Mail to:
Safer Society Press
PO Box 340, Brandon, VT 05733-0340

For SSF use only

Shipping & Handling

1-5 items	$5	26-30 items	$18
6-10 items	$8	31-35 items	$22
11-15 items	$10	36-40 items	$25
16-20 items	$12	41-50 items	$30
21-25 items	$15	51 + items	$35

Call for quote on rush orders

Phone orders with
MasterCard or Visa
Call (802) 247-3132